Math in Motion

FIRST STEPS IN MUSIC THEORY

tip
** Pay attention to
almost every detail
and don't be shy to ask
what may seem like obvious
questions*

SECOND EDITION

*! and do the EXs
by yourself! don't
skip stuff!*

Caleb Skogen

WITH KYLE BAILEY

MULTIMEDIA

Caleb Skogen with Kyle Bailey, *Math in Motion: First Steps in Music Theory*, 2nd edition

© 2017 Classical Conversations® MultiMedia, Inc. All rights reserved. First edition published 2015.

Published by Classical Conversations® MultiMedia, Inc.
255 Air Tool Drive
Southern Pines, NC 28387

www.ClassicalConversations.com | www.ClassicalConversationsBooks.com

Cover design by Classical Conversations. Cover image: *Music and Literature*, William Michael Harnett, 1878. Courtesy of the Albright-Knox Art Gallery, public domain.

All Scripture quotations, unless otherwise noted, are taken from the King James Version of the Bible.

Printed in the United States of America

ISBN: 978-0-9984373-5-4

Table of Contents

Beware
hard
easy

Introduction

Although we seldom think about it, the connection between math and music is as natural as the connection between math and science. After all, as philosopher Gottfried Leibniz put it, "Music is the pleasure the human mind experiences from counting without being aware that it is counting." Without math, music loses all sense of rhythm, and it is rhythm (even if it is changed or delayed) that distinguishes music from cacophony.

And yet, rhythm isn't the only mathematical component of music. What about tone? The measurable frequencies of sound waves allow us to recognize notes. In addition, the fixed distances between notes make melody and harmony both possible and appealing.

It is little wonder then that when the leaders of the medieval university system defined the quadrivium, they described math as pure number and music as math in motion.

By beginning the study of music theory from a mathematical perspective, we are giving students the opportunity to experience the kind of wonder that often arises after close examination of an object. For example, we might observe a pond that is teeming with fish, insects, frogs, and turtles, but it is not until we examine a drop of pond water under a microscope that we truly gain an appreciation for the abundance of living things that call the pond home.

In the same way, once students understand the structure of music better, they can notice and appreciate more about the music they encounter every day. And, they can begin to contemplate big ideas such as "How is music beautiful?" or "What does it mean to create beautiful works?"

Math in Motion will cover foundational concepts in music theory and how these concepts relate to written pieces of music. The primary focus is a specific part of music theory called score analysis.

It is important to note that there are aspects of music theory that this text will not cover fully. For example, while rhythm is an extremely important element of music, the scope of this text prevents a full treatment of it. The student may be left with questions about rhythm, but that is the point. When questions pique curiosity, a student will be more likely to take learning into his or her own hands. Such is the goal of any classical curriculum.

It is helpful if students either begin or continue to play an instrument while going through this book. That way, the forms of music theory can be discovered (or rediscovered) within the context of study. However, if you do not have any musical training, do not worry—this book is for you too!

The Goal

"What is happening in this music?" This important question provides the central theme for this textbook. *Math in Motion* seeks to teach the foundations of music through analysis of hymn scores to help students understand what is going on behind the music they hear.

Exercises

Each chapter is designed to introduce a new concept of music theory. The in-class activities will help students understand the material and prepare for the exercises they will do for homework.

Many of the exercises use excerpts from the six scores that are found at the end of the book. These scores are important tools in teaching score analysis, which builds toward the end-of-semester project. Get to know these scores!

Terms

Important terms are written in bold when the term is introduced so the student may find them more easily when review is needed. These terms are also in the glossary.

Helpful Tools

In the back of the book there are tools that will be helpful for completing exercises and reviewing core concepts. Included in this section are blank staff paper, keyboards, note names, note values, and the Circle of Fifths diagram.

Let's Get Started

Be curious about the possibilities of music. Be curious about this art, this science, this gift that plays a pivotal role in every culture in the world. A wonderful opportunity lies ahead of you in the pages of *Math in Motion*!

Music is enough for a whole lifetime—but a lifetime is not enough for music.

—Sergei Rachmaninoff, 1956

Acknowledgments

This book began primarily with Leigh Bortins and the students of the first class of Mandala Fellowship. Teaching harmonics at Mandala Fellowship provided a stimulating environment for me to explore and learn how to teach music theory. I have profited greatly from working with Leigh Bortins on a daily basis. She draws out excellent work from everyone around her, and I hold her in high regard. Thank you, Leigh, for your trust in me, your encouragement, and your contagious passion for learning that still influences me today. Thank you also to those students at Mandala who put up with my many mistakes, who challenged me, and who also encouraged me to be a better teacher and person for the sake of others.

I am honored to write a music theory curriculum for Classical Conversations. The Classical Conversations team offered helpful advice and guidance. I especially want to thank Jen Greenholt for her kindness and encouragement throughout the writing process. It was a privilege to work with her, and I hope to have many more opportunities to work with and learn from her.

As the book took structure, Kate Deddens, Shelly Stockton, Jennifer Courtney, and Michael Healey offered insight and support. Thanks are also due to Anna Gissing and Cyndi Widman, whose attention to detail gave the book its cohesiveness. Thank you also to those who piloted the curriulum and who worked diligently to offer their feedback and wisdom. I especially want to thank Chelly Barnard for all of her persistence to make the book more accessible for students. I am greatly indebted to all of them and the hard work they put forth in completing this project. Throughout the development of this book, I learned from many other authors who have published works on music theory, including Jonathan Harnum, Joseph N. Straus, Victor Zuckerkandl, Aaron Copland, and Jeremy Begbie.

I was also fortunate to work with our graphic designer, Kathi James, who has a wonderful ability to make any content look better than it is. She amazes me with her gift of artistry and creativity, and I happily admit this book would be lacking without her touch.

The largest expression of gratitude goes to my wife, Catie. More than anyone, she has encouraged me to seek God through my passion for music and has truly been a wonderful source of motivation and inspiration. I would not love music or others as much as I do without her help.

—CDS

Many thanks to Kyle Bailey, Adjunct Professor of Music Theory at Liberty University, as well as Chelly Barnard, Kathy Donegia, and Marc Hays, Academic Advisors with Classical Conversations, for their efforts on this second edition. Their dedication and attention to detail made this work possible.

I used to think that music was like lace upon a garment, nice to have but not necessary. I have come to believe that music is absolutely essential to our community life.

—George Eastman, 1956

1 Fundamentals of Music: Pitch

Music is a language and, like all languages, it is meant to communicate ideas. In order for any language to work, however, we as listeners must understand the rules that describe it, or its "grammar." We begin our study of music with grammar.

The most basic element of musical grammar is music notation. Even though there are many different styles of instrumentation, music notation is key to both playing and understanding music.

Music notation tells us many things about a piece of music, but the most foundational information it gives us is about pitch. **Pitch** is the attribute of a musical tone produced by the number of vibrations generating it. Pitch can be high or low. As we explore the idea of pitch we will encounter many different concepts: the musical staff, treble and bass clefs, and note names. This chapter aims to discuss these and other foundational aspects through activities and exercises. This foundation will allow you to understand the additional music theory concepts introduced later in all their orderly beauty.

Notes on the Keyboard

Of all the variety of instruments, the keyboard is the most helpful for learning the concepts of music theory, especially notation, since it helps you to visualize and remember the structure of music. Even if you do not have a keyboard or piano in your home, you can still learn about music theory. For this curriculum, you will need only the diagrams on the page, though you may wish to add a practical component by using a physical keyboard or one of the virtual keyboards readily accessible online.

[Music] takes us out of the actual and whispers to us dim secrets that startle our wonder as to (what) who we are and for what, whence, and whereto. All the great interrogatories like questioning Angels float in on its waves of sound.
—Ralph Waldo Emerson

Figure 1.1

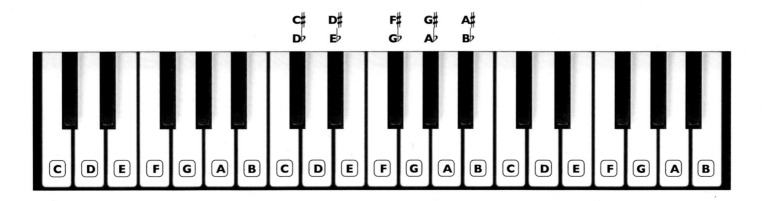

In Figure 1.1, you can see every note that exists in modern Western music theory. The notes of a keyboard have higher pitches when moving right (up) and lower pitches when moving left (down).

A keyboard or piano has black and white keys. The white keys are named with the first seven letters of the alphabet: **A, B, C, D, E, F,** and **G.** These notes are called **natural notes.** Natural notes repeat themselves in alphabetical order up and down the keyboard. The groupings of the black keys in twos and threes help the eye see the differences between the locations of each white key. For example, C is always immediately below (to the left of) the first black key in the group of two. The F is always immediately below (to the left of) the first black key in the group of three. Refer to Figure 1.2 below.

Figure 1.2

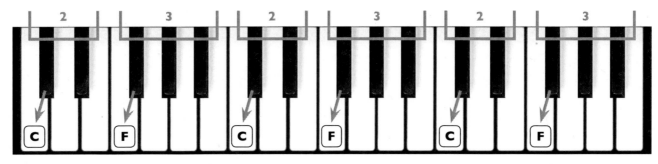

As you can see, the natural notes are represented by the letter names A, B, C, D, E, F, and G. You are probably wondering how to notate the black keys. The black keys on a keyboard can be identified by two important symbols: a **flat** (♭) or a **sharp** (♯). Sharps and flats alter the pitch of a note by one half step, going either up (♯) or down (♭). The **natural** (♮) is used to cancel out either a sharp or a flat to indicate that the note is in its natural state. These three symbols are called **accidentals**.

A **half step** is the shortest distance between two notes. The distance between E natural and E♭ (the note immediately to the left of E on a keyboard) is one half step. The distance between B and C (the note immediately to the right of B on a keyboard) is one half step. In essence, a half step describes the distance between a given note and the next available note higher or lower.

A **whole step** is the distance of pitch equal to two half steps. For example, the distance between F and G is a whole step. A whole step, therefore, describes the distance between a given note and two half steps higher or lower.

sharp

natural

flat

Figure 1.3

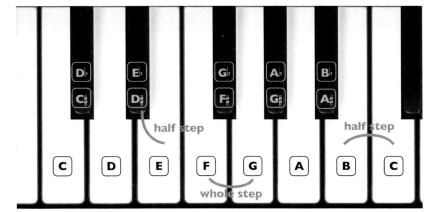

BONUS

Sharp (♯), flat (♭), and natural (♮) symbols are called accidentals.

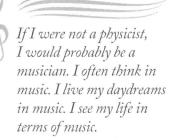

If I were not a physicist, I would probably be a musician. I often think in music. I live my daydreams in music. I see my life in terms of music.

—Albert Einstein

A flat indicates the note is lowered (moved left) one half step. For example, the note G♭ is positioned one half step to the left (down) from G♮. The flat signifies the shift downward to the next available note.

A sharp indicates the note is raised (moved right) one half step. For example, take a look at the position of F♯ on the keyboard in Figure 1.3. Its position immediately to the right of F♮ indicates that it is one half step higher than F♮.

Figure 1.4

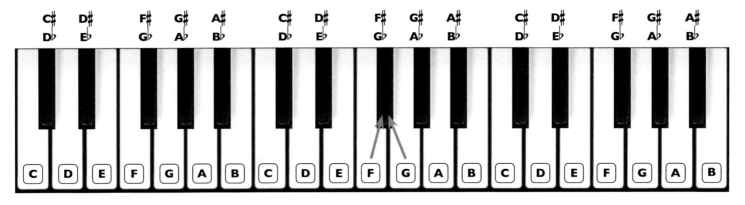

You have likely noticed in Figure 1.4 that the notes discussed above, F♯ and G♭, are on the same black key. In fact, each of the black keys, and some white keys, have two different names. When two notes have the same pitch or tone, but different names, the names are said to be **enharmonic equivalents** of each other. For example, C♯ is one half step higher than C♮, so it can be called C♯. However, it is also one half step lower than D♮, so it can also be called D♭. In theory, every note has an enharmonic equivalent.

White keys can have enharmonic equivalents, too. For example, in Figure 1.5 the note to the right of E can be called F, but it can also be called E♯. The note that is to the left of C can be called B, but it can also be called C♭. The rule of enharmonic equivalents holds whether the keys are black or white.

Figure 1.5

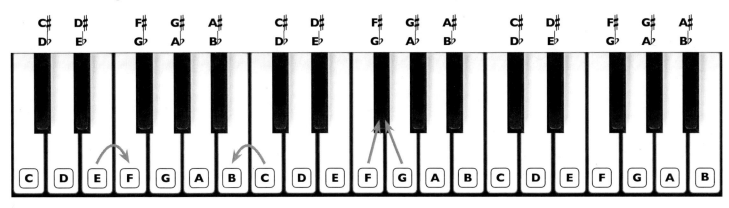

Activity 1.1—In-class activity

a) Write in the name of the notes on the blank lines you see on the keyboard in
    Figure 1.6.

b) If all the responses you provided in Figure 1.6 were lowered one half step (flatted),
    what would the names of the notes be?

c) If all the responses you provided in Figure 1.6 were raised one half step (sharped),
    what would the names of the notes be?

d) Name the enharmonic equivalents of each of the black keys, labeled a–d below.

Figure 1.6

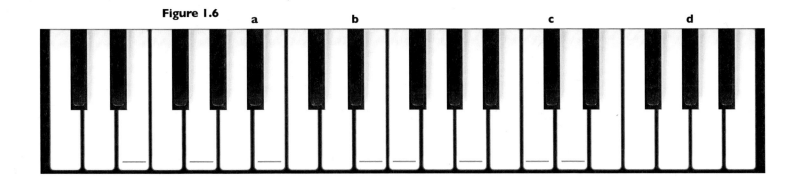

clef: (from Middle French) a figurative term derived from the classical Latin word *clavis*, meaning "a literal key, such as one that would open doors"

Notes on the Staff

Figure 1.7

Musical notes are written on a five-line **staff** (plural, staves) (Figure 1.7). The notes can be written on the lines or in the spaces between the lines of the staff. These lines and spaces represent different notes. However, this staff is unable to denote pitches without a musical symbol known as a clef. **Clefs** are characters set at the head of the staff to indicate the pitch or position of the notes.

treble clef: a symbol used to notate pitches that are to be played on a higher pitched instrument or with the right hand on a keyboard. This is also called the G clef because this symbol evolved from the letter G.

bass clef: a symbol used to notate pitches that are to be played on a lower pitched instrument or with the left hand on a keyboard. This is also called the F clef because this symbol evolved from the letter F. (Note: In music, "bass" is pronounced as "base," like in "baseball," not like the fish.)

Notation on Treble and Bass Clefs

In order to understand music theory, you must learn the names of the notes on the treble and bass clefs. Thankfully, you can use phrases and acronyms to help memorize the notes that correspond to each line and space of the staff.

BONUS

Figure 1.8

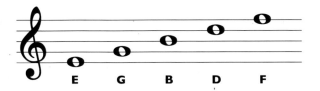 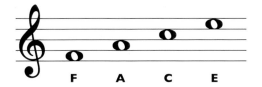

Notice how the curve of the treble clef always encircles the line for the note G.

In Figure 1.8, the names of the notes on the lines and spaces of the treble clef are written out. The notes on the lines are E, G, B, D, and F, which you can memorize using this phrase: **E**very **G**ood **B**oy **D**oes **F**ine.

The notes on the spaces of the treble clef are F, A, C, and E, which you can memorize by recognizing that they spell **FACE**.

Figure 1.9

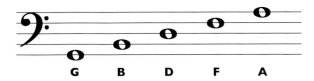 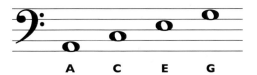

Notice how the two dots of the bass clef always surround the line for the note F.

In Figure 1.9, the names of the notes on the lines and spaces of the bass clef are written out. The notes on the lines are G, B, D, F, and A, which you can memorize using this phrase: **G**ood **B**oys **D**o **F**ine **A**lways.

The notes on the spaces of the bass clef are A, C, E, and G, which you can memorize using this phrase: **A**ll **C**ows **E**at **G**rass.

Ledger lines are used to show notes that go higher or lower than the five lines of the staff. In Figures 1.8 and 1.9 we show only the names of notes that are within the lines and spaces of the staff. However, ledger lines, shown in Figure 1.10, can be added for notes that go higher than the top line of a staff and lower than the bottom line of a staff. When you move higher or lower than the top or bottom of the staff, you simply continue the note names. For example, the top note on the treble clef is F. If you go to the next space above it, the note is a G. If you continue upward and add a ledger line, the name of the note is A.

Figure 1.10 Ledger lines

Octaves

An **octave** is the distance between two notes with the same letter name (including sharps and flats). As we stated earlier in the chapter, the pattern of notes (A, B, C, D, E, F, G) repeats in both directions: higher and lower. However, in order to help us discuss the location between the different octaves, we use register designations, which denote the letter name of the note plus a number. These numbers are derived from the note's position on the piano from left to right. Look at Figure 1.11 and notice the letters with the register designations. Observe how the lowest C is named C1 and how the distance between C1 and C2 is one octave. Since C1 to C2 is an octave, then C1 to C3 is two octaves, and so on. As you review Figure 1.11, also notice that the numbers change at C; for example, all of the letter names between C2 and C3 have the number 2 as their designation.

*Octave charting only starts on C1. The notes below C1 (B, B♭, and A) are not included in octave charts.

Figure 1.11

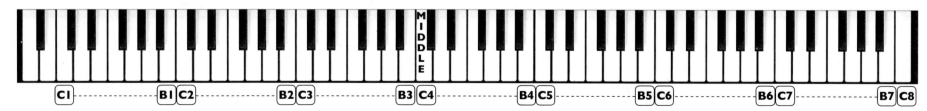

BONUS

The symbol *8va* is an abbreviation of the Italian word for octave, *ottava* (pronounced oh-TAH-vah). *Otta* is the Italian feminine of "eight."

The Keyboard

In sheet music, the keyboard uses both treble and bass clefs that are joined together to make up a **grand staff**. On the grand staff, an important component is **middle C**. Middle C is the first ledger line below the treble clef and the first ledger line above the bass clef. On the piano, it is near the middle of the keyboard, with twenty-three white keys to the left and twenty-eight white keys to the right. Look at Figure 1.12 to see how the notes of a keyboard are notated on both the treble and bass clefs. Do you see middle C?

Often, middle C will be a general dividing line between which area of the keyboard should be played with the right hand and which with the left.

Figure 1.12

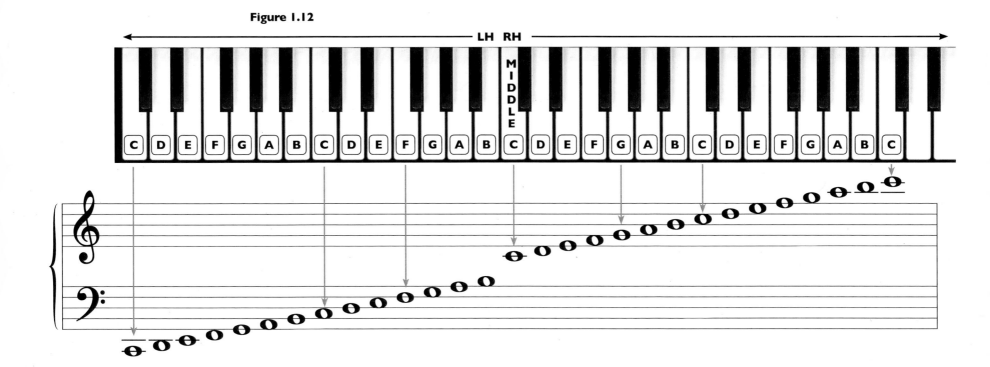

Chapter 1 Review

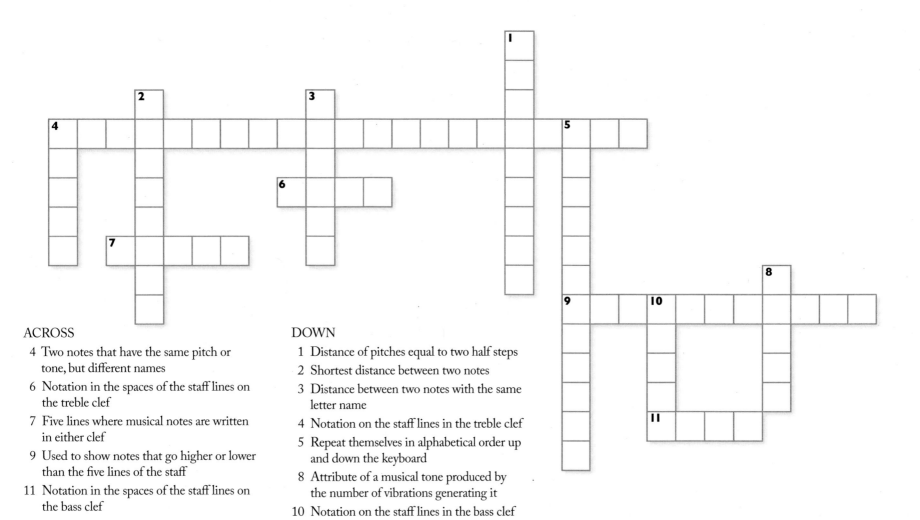

ACROSS

4 Two notes that have the same pitch or tone, but different names

6 Notation in the spaces of the staff lines on the treble clef

7 Five lines where musical notes are written in either clef

9 Used to show notes that go higher or lower than the five lines of the staff

11 Notation in the spaces of the staff lines on the bass clef

DOWN

1 Distance of pitches equal to two half steps

2 Shortest distance between two notes

3 Distance between two notes with the same letter name

4 Notation on the staff lines in the treble clef

5 Repeat themselves in alphabetical order up and down the keyboard

8 Attribute of a musical tone produced by the number of vibrations generating it

10 Notation on the staff lines in the bass clef

Daily Exercises for Chapter 1

❧ EXERCISES FOR DAY 1

Re-read chapter 1 and complete the following exercises:

Exercise 1.1

Provide the letter names for each specified key marked on the keyboard.

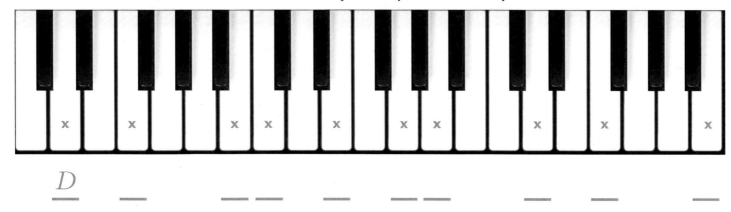

D ___ ___ ___ ___ ___ ___ ___ ___ ___ ___ ___ ___

Exercise 1.2

Provide the name for each black key marked on the keyboard and include its enharmonic equivalent name.

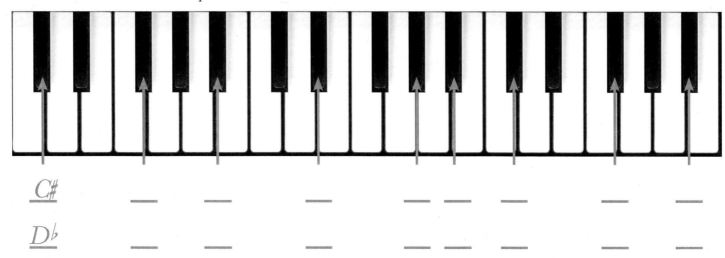

$C\#$ ___ ___ ___ ___ ___ ___ ___ ___

$D\flat$ ___ ___ ___ ___ ___ ___ ___ ___

Exercise 1.3

Use arrows to show motions of whole or half steps above the given note.

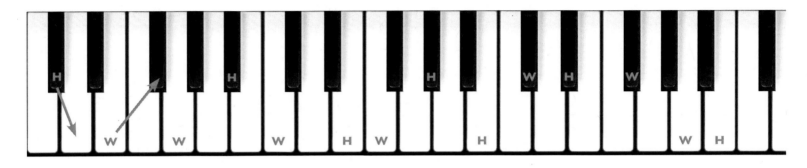

Exercise 1.4

On the staff below, write a flat in front of the first four notes, a sharp in front of the next four notes, and a natural in front of the final four notes.

Exercise 1.5

Give the note enharmonically equivalent to each of the following notes:

a) B♯ _____   b) D♭ _____   c) E♮ _____   d) E♭ _____

e) G♯ _____   f) A♭ _____   g) F♯ _____   h) C♮ _____

  EXERCISES FOR DAY 2

Re-read chapter 1 and complete the following exercises:

Exercise 1.6

Practice drawing the symbols for a treble and bass clef on the following staves (plural of "staff").

Bonus: Try using a calligraphy pen to achieve the broader and narrower sections of the lines.

Exercise 1.7

Name the following notes on the treble clef:

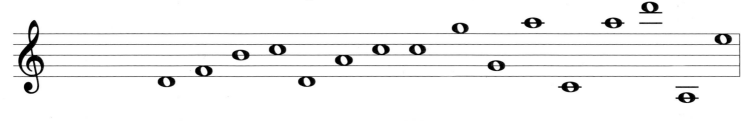

Name the following notes on the bass clef:

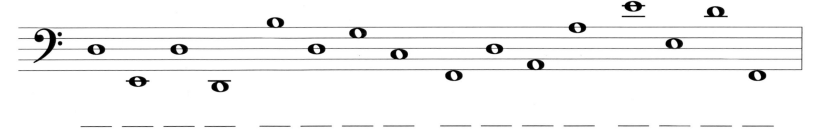

__ __ __ __ __ __ __ __ __ __ __ __ __ __

Exercise 1.8

Draw arrows from the treble clef set of notes to the correct key on the keyboard.

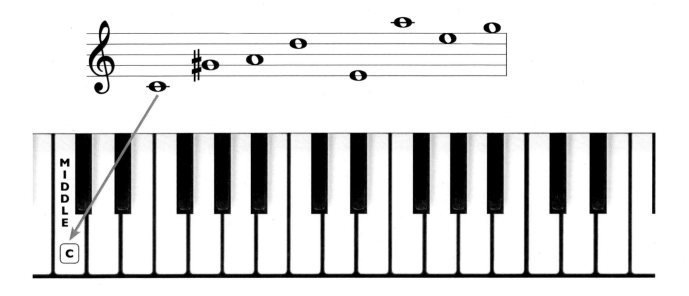

Draw arrows from the bass clef set of notes to the correct key on the keyboard.

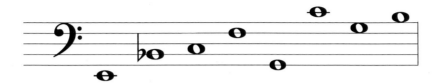

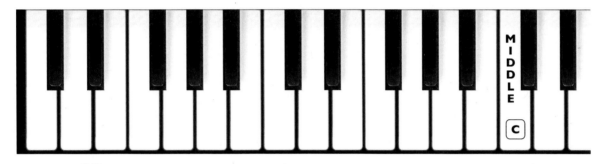

✵ EXERCISES FOR DAY 3

The figures in the following exercises are excerpts from the scores at the end of your book. Refer to the scores to guide you through these exercises.

Exercise 1.9

The following excerpt is the third line on the treble clef of the hymn "When Peace Like a River." Label these notes with the correct note names.

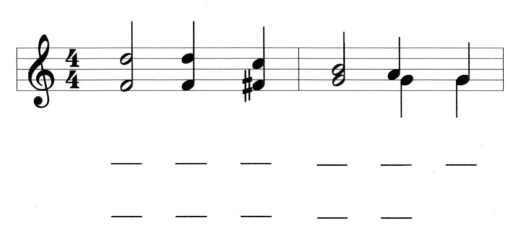

B O N U S

TIP: This illustration contains quarter notes and half notes. You will learn more about them in chapter 2. For now, just focus on the placement of the notes on the staff, not on the shapes of the notes.

Exercise 1.10

The following excerpt is the third line on the bass clef of the hymn "When Peace Like a River." Identify the numbered notes by writing their numbers on the keyboard below.

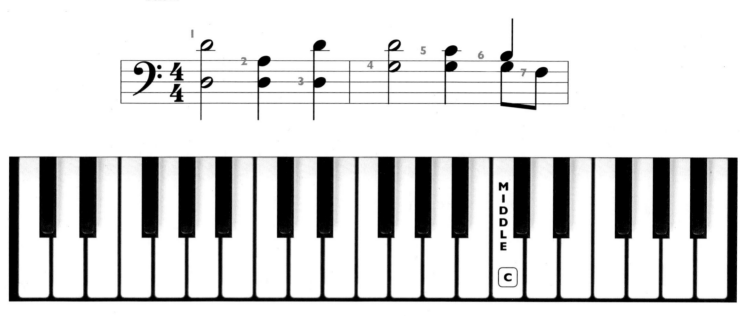

♒ EXERCISES FOR DAY 4

Exercise 1.11

Write the following notes on the treble clef (there can be more than one correct answer). The first one is done for you with all possible answers.

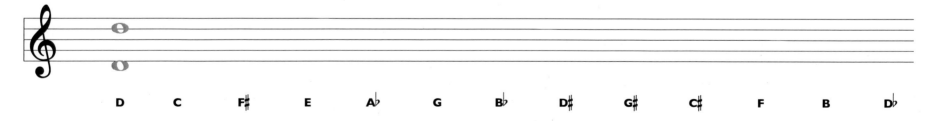

D   C   F♯   E   A♭   G   B♭   D♯   G♯   C♯   F   B   D♭

Exercise 1.12

Write the following notes on the bass clef:

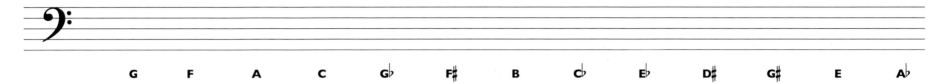

Exercise 1.13

Draw arrows from the notes on the staff to their corresponding keys on the keyboard (MC = middle C).

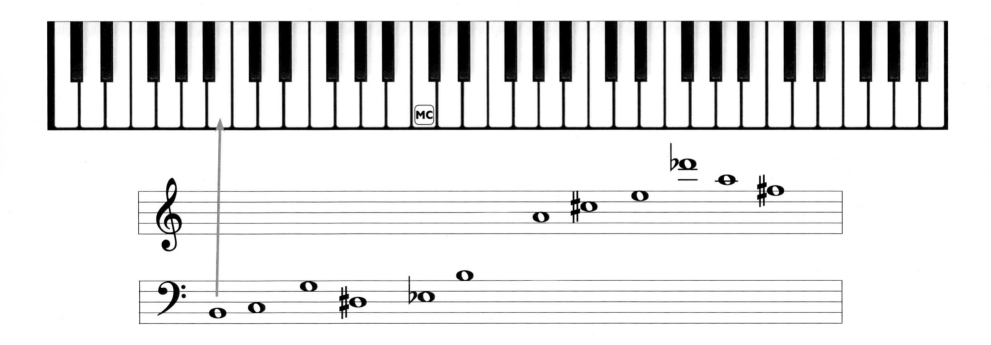

Exercise 1.14

Notate each note with an "x" on the staff provided below. Once notated, draw arrows from the keys on the keyboard to their corresponding notes on the staff (MC = middle C).

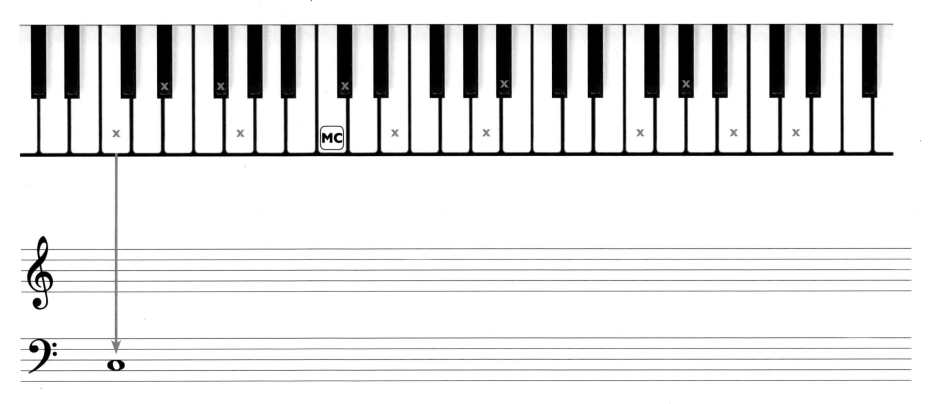

Exercise 1.15

Use the keyboard below to mark the following keys and specific octaves:

a) Label all of the C keys on the keyboard with a C directly below each key.

b) Label all of the F♯ keys on the keyboard with an F♯ directly above each key.

c) Label all the G octaves on the keyboard with a G and the correct register designation on each key.

d) Label all the E octaves on the keyboard with an E and the correct register designation on each key.

e) Mark the keys on the keyboard that do not belong to any octave charts by writing an "x" on the keys.

2 Introduction to Rhythm

In the last chapter, we discussed pitch, an important component of all music. However, pitch is only one piece of what is needed to create music. The other component, **rhythm**, can be understood as the passage of pitch through time. "Rhythm" comes from the Latin word *rhythmus,* meaning "movement in time." In music, rhythm is when pitches are played or heard within the movement of time. Without rhythm, the mix of different sounds would have no structure and there would be no music. Genres of music differ more in their rhythms than in any other element.

Before we can discuss how to notate and create pitch through time, we start by learning the symbols used to express rhythm.

Note Values

The specific duration of a note—the length of time the note is played—is called its **note value**. For the purpose of this text, there are five basic symbols for note value: the whole note, half note, quarter note, eighth note, and sixteenth note.

Figure 2.1

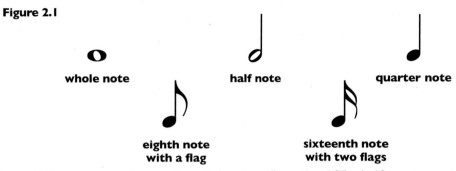

The **whole note** resembles a circle, called an "open" note head. The **half note** is similar to the whole note, as it too contains an open note head, but there is also a new element: a stem. By adding the stem to the existing whole note, it becomes a half note. The **quarter note** is similar to the half note, as it has a stem and note head, but the note head is "filled in" rather than open.

The stems can point up or down. Typically, the lower notes on the staff have stems pointing up from the right side of the note head, and the higher notes on the staff have stems pointing down from the left side of the note head.

Figure 2.2

The **eighth note** is closely related to the quarter note, as it has a filled-in note head and a stem, but it also has a flag. The flag is always written to the right of the stem, whether the stem is pointing up or down.

Figure 2.3 Eighth notes with flags and eighth notes with beams

When more than one eighth note is present, the flag can be replaced by a beam. We will discuss beams in chapters 3 and 4; for now, it is sufficient to know that one beam connecting two notes communicates that the note values are eighth notes.

The **sixteenth note** is written with a filled-in note head and a stem that includes two flags that are always written to the right of the stem. Sixteenth notes can also be written with connecting beams, and, just as they have two flags, they also have two beams.

Figure 2.4 Sixteenth notes with flags and sixteenth notes with beams

Activity 2.1—In-class activity

Write four of each of the following note values on the staves below:

1) Whole notes
2) Half notes
3) Quarter notes
4) Eighth notes with a flag
5) Eighth note pairs beamed together
6) Sixteenth notes with two flags
7) Sixteenth note pairs beamed together

Metric Hierarchy

Note values have a very specific relationship built upon the division of two from the greatest note value. The whole note has the greatest value. When we divide it into two equal parts, a half note is created. One half note is half of the value of the whole note. When we divide the half note into two equal parts, a quarter note is created. Each quarter note is half the value of the half note and one quarter the value of the whole note. We can continue this hierarchy by dividing the quarter note into two parts to create the eighth note, and subsequently the sixteenth note.

Figure 2.5

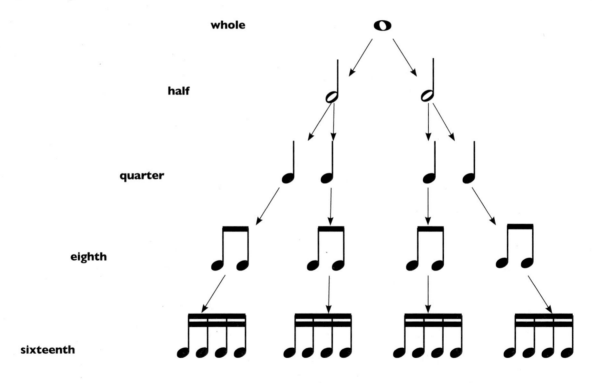

Rest and Note Comparison

The rhythm symbols discussed thus far let the composer create pitches that have a specific duration, but music is more than just pitches with rhythm; it also includes breaks or silences in the music. These breaks are called rests. A **rest** requires a specific time of silence using symbols that correspond to note values. Whereas a note requires that a pitch be held for a certain amount of time, a rest requires silence for a certain amount of time. Look at the following examples of rests and their corresponding note values.

[Music] is the "arithmetic of sound" just as optics is the "geometry of light."

—Claude Debussy, c. 1900

Figure 2.6

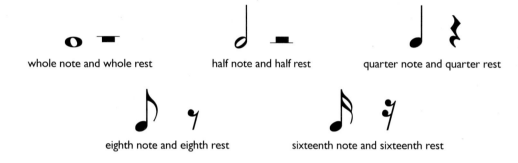

whole note and whole rest   half note and half rest   quarter note and quarter rest

eighth note and eighth rest   sixteenth note and sixteenth rest

Dotted and Tied Notes

There are two basic ways to increase the value of a given note or rest: an augmentation dot and a tie.

The **augmentation dot** is placed directly after a note or rest and increases the note value of a note or rest by half. For example, suppose the augmentation dot is placed after a quarter note. Half the value of the quarter note is added to the existing duration, creating a note value that is equal to a quarter note and an eighth note (or three eighths).

Figure 2.7

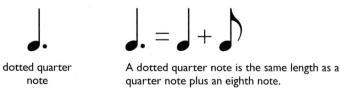

dotted quarter note

A dotted quarter note is the same length as a quarter note plus an eighth note.

Another way to increase the value of a given note is with a tie. A **tie** is a curved line connecting two notes of the same pitch that are to be sounded as one note equal to their combined note value. Ties are used to prolong notes of the same pitch. Figure 2.8 below is an example of a quarter note tied to a half note. When a note is tied to another note, it does not mean to play the note twice. Instead, the lengths of the two notes are added together so that the note is prolonged, or extended. A tie is always drawn from note head to note head as illustrated in Figure 2.8, not from stem to stem.

Figure 2.8

If the note were played on a piano, the key would be held down the total length of the notes added together. In Figure 2.9, the length of the two notes would equal a dotted half note.

Figure 2.9

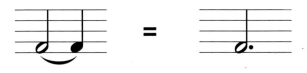

Chapter 2 Review

```
H  A  L  F  N  O  T  E  V  D  K  R  P  U  A  E  I  T
F  M  R  E  S  I  K  G  U  E  W  F  H  U  F  Q  R  S
F  Q  O  G  C  K  N  U  L  E  R  W  G  Y  M  I  H  E
E  H  C  U  U  L  X  T  E  T  W  M  D  S  T  S  L  T
W  T  I  N  F  U  W  C  C  O  E  N  X  T  I  H  R  S
Z  G  O  E  T  O  N  H  T  N  E  E  T  X  I  S  M  E
C  E  C  N  F  Q  Q  W  T  H  W  A  P  T  W  G  T  R
J  N  B  G  R  A  A  A  S  T  C  N  S  Z  J  O  Q  R
L  Z  C  Q  Z  E  T  V  N  H  Y  O  O  F  N  I  F  E
F  E  J  H  V  I  T  L  I  G  J  F  U  E  Y  P  G  T
W  W  S  T  O  N  H  R  P  I  B  W  L  P  W  V  A  R
H  W  H  N  B  N  E  O  A  E  W  O  P  U  Q  N  M  A
A  V  D  C  M  E  H  H  O  U  H  M  G  H  F  V  J  U
Q  O  P  J  V  E  J  X  Y  W  Q  C  K  B  V  K  E  Q
T  R  C  Y  M  E  V  Y  Z  N  R  Q  I  E  U  I  X  Q
X  C  J  H  V  B  R  X  K  E  A  T  A  A  J  Q  B  G
N  R  H  P  W  B  G  P  S  H  N  Z  F  M  A  X  H  I
D  R  C  Z  F  M  P  T  S  M  J  G  E  A  P  I  S  F
```

1 A dot placed directly after a note to increase the note value of a note or rest by half of the note value

2 A bar that replaces the flag to connect two eighth notes

3 ♪

4 ♩

5 𝄽

6 The passage of pitch through time

7 ♪

8 Curved line connecting two note heads used to prolong notes of the same pitch

9 𝅝

Daily Exercises for Chapter 2

 EXERCISES FOR DAY 1

Read through chapter 2 and complete the following exercises:

Exercise 2.1

On the staff below write two whole notes, four half notes, and four quarter notes.
(The stem, if needed, can go either up or down.)

Exercise 2.2

On the staff below write six eighth notes with flags, three groupings of two eighth notes beamed together, six sixteenth notes with flags, and three groupings of two sixteenth notes beamed together. (The stem, if needed, can go either up or down.)

𝄢𝄐 EXERCISES FOR DAY 2

Review chapter 2 and complete the following exercises:

Exercise 2.3

Answer the following questions and prepare to do some math:

a) How many half notes make up one whole note?

b) How many quarter notes make up one half note?

c) How many eighth notes make up one half note?

d) How many sixteenth notes make up one whole note?

e) How many sixteenth notes make up four eighth notes?

f) How many eighth notes make up four half notes?

g) How many quarter notes make up four whole notes?

h) Thirty-two sixteenth notes make up how many whole notes?

i) Sixteen quarter notes make up how many half notes?

j) Thirty-two eighth notes make up how many half notes?

Exercise 2.4

Write a note equal to the following sets of notes.

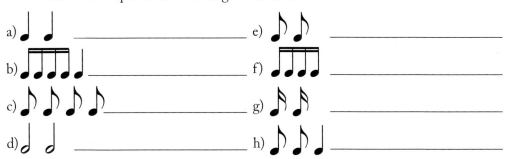

EXERCISES FOR DAY 3

Review chapter 2 and complete the following exercises:

Exercise 2.5

Write two notes whose combined value is equal to the following sets of notes:

a) 𝅝 = _____ + _____   d) ♪ = _____ + _____

b) 𝅗𝅥 = _____ + _____   e) ♩ = _____ + _____

c) ♪♪♪♪ = _____ + _____   f) ♫ ♫ = _____ + _____

Exercise 2.6

Draw the corresponding rest sign next to the following notes:

a) ♪ = _____   d) 𝅘𝅥𝅯 = _____

b) 𝅝 = _____   e) 𝅗𝅥 = _____

c) ♩ = _____

Exercise 2.7

Draw a single rest equal to the following sets of notes:

a) ♪♪♪♪ ♩ = _____   e) 𝅗𝅥 𝅗𝅥 = _____

b) ♪ ♪ = _____   f) ♩ ♪♪♪♪ 𝅗𝅥 = _____

c) ♪ ♪ ♪ ♪ = _____   g) ♩ ♩ = _____

d) 𝅘𝅥𝅯 𝅘𝅥𝅯 = _____   h) ♪ ♪ ♩ = _____

EXERCISES FOR DAY 4

Review chapter 2 and complete the following exercises:

Exercise 2.8

Write two notes or rests whose combined value is equal to the following sets of dotted notes and rests. Use notes when notes are given; use rests when rests are given.

1. 𝅗𝅥. = _____ + _____

2. ♩. = _____ + _____

3. ▬. = _____ + _____

4. ▬. = _____ + _____

5. 𝅝. = _____ + _____

6. ♪. = _____ + _____

7. 𝄽. = _____ + _____

8. 𝄾. = _____ + _____

Exercise 2.9

Given the tied notes below, write a single note of equal value.

1.   =   _____

2.   =   _____

3.   =   _____

4.   =   _____

5.   =   _____

6.   =   _____

3 Simple Meter

In the preceding chapter, we introduced basic rhythm by studying the different notes, rests, and their relative values. But what determines their different values and how they fit together in the broader context of a musical work? This chapter will expand our grammar of rhythm through both examples and practice.

Foundations of Meter

Let's begin with the smallest metrical unit in music, the beat. The **beat** is the fixed, rhythmic pulse of a piece of music. All of music is "felt" or experienced in terms of the beat. Much like your own heartbeat, the beat provides a consistent pulse for the music. The beat in music consists of two elements: the beat groupings (a specific number of beats grouped together) and the beat divisions (equal fractional parts of the beat). When the same number of beat groupings occurs repeatedly throughout a piece of music, we call it **meter**. Meter describes the specific beat groupings and divisions that occur within music. A singular grouping of beats is called a **measure**. A vertical line called a **bar line** separates one measure from another on the staff.

Figure 3.1

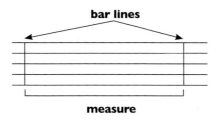

bar lines

measure

Nothing exists without music; for the universe itself is said to have been framed by a kind of harmony of sounds, and the heaven itself revolves under the tones of that harmony.

—Isidore of Seville

Meter, therefore, allows the composer to create music with a certain expressive quality. This quality is expressed through a specific number of beats per measure and a particular number of divisions of the beat.

There are two basic types of meter: simple and compound. **Simple meter** is defined as a meter in which the beat is divided into two equal parts. **Compound meter** is defined as a meter in which the beat is divided into three equal parts.

Understanding Meter

To understand this idea, let's look at two familiar pieces: "Twinkle, Twinkle, Little Star," and, "Row, Row, Row Your Boat." In addition to the figures below, you will need to hear a recording of each piece. You can find many examples on the Internet to aid you in this section.

Figure 3.2

Twin-kle, twin-kle, lit-tle star, how I won-der what you are.
beat   beat   beat   beat beat   beat   beat   beat

As you review the lyrics and listen to a recording of "Twinkle, Twinkle, Little Star" (Figure 3.2), tap along with the music. As you tap, you should "feel" the beat on the lyrics and syllables *Twin-, twin-, lit-, star, how, won-, what,* and *are.* If we inspect the beat while listening more closely, we find that each one of those beats is divided into two equal parts. In fact, the missing syllables of the lyrics demonstrate this as they are even between every beat. When we look at this piece, we see the beat on the syllable "twin-" and the note in-between the beat on "-kle." This note between the beats is called subdivision of the beat. Because the beats in "Twinkle, Twinkle, Little Star," can be subdivided by two, this is an example of simple meter.

Figure 3.3

Row, row, row your boat, gent-ly down the stream.
beat   beat   beat   beat   beat   beat   beat

Mer-ri-ly, mer-ri-ly, mer-ri-ly, mer-ri-ly
beat   beat   beat   beat

If you tap the beat while listening to a recording of "Row, Row, Row Your Boat" (Figure 3.3), you should find that the beat occurs on the lyrics and syllables *Row, row, row, boat, gen-, down, stream, Mer-, mer-, mer-,* and *mer-*. Upon closer inspection, you will find that each one of those beats is divided into three equal parts. This is most noticeable in the way we hear the word *merrily*. We see the beat on the syllable *mer-* and the notes between the beat on the syllables *-ri* and *-ly*. Because the beats in "Row, Row, Row Your Boat" can be subdivided into three parts, this is an example of compound meter.

Time Signatures

The abstract idea of meter can be represented by a **time signature**. This vertical stack of numbers is placed at the beginning of the staff immediately following the clef to indicate the meter. Based upon whether the meter is simple or compound, it gives specific information about the music, including the beat, subdivision of the beat, and number of beats.

Figure 3.4

When a time signature represents simple meter, it gives information about the beat. But, when a time signature represents compound meter, it gives information about the subdivisions of the beat. It is very important that we differentiate between meter types before assessing time signatures. There is a basic observation we can make that will help us

BONUS

Sometimes there is less than a full measure at the beginning of a piece of music. When this happens, the extra beats are called an **anacrusis**. They are also commonly referred to as pick-up notes. See the scores for "There Is a Fountain" and "When Peace Like a River" for examples.

distinguish between meter types: the top number of the time signature. If the top number of the time signature is 2, 3, or 4, it represents simple meter—a beat division of two. If the top number of the time signature is 6, 9, or 12, it represents compound meter, where the beat is divided into three equal parts.

Figure 3.5

Top Number of Time Signature	Meter Type	Number of Beat Divisions
2	simple	two
3	simple	two
4	simple	two
6	compound	three
9	compound	three
12	compound	three

Activity 3.1 — In-class activity

Identify the different types of meter (simple or compound) given the time signatures below:

$\frac{6}{8}$ _____ $\frac{9}{16}$ _____

$\frac{4}{4}$ _____ $\frac{12}{4}$ _____

$\frac{2}{8}$ _____ $\frac{3}{4}$ _____

[Music is] a kind of counting performed by the mind without knowing that it is counting.

—Gottfried Wilhelm Leibniz

Simple Meter and Time Signatures

While the previous section has served as a basic introduction to meter, both simple and compound, we will deal exclusively with simple meter for the remainder of the chapter. Compound meter, and thus the time signatures that represent it, will be discussed in chapter 4.

As we have already discussed, when the top number of a given time signature is a 2, 3, or 4, the meter it represents is simple. When a time signature represents simple meter, it gives two important pieces of information: the number of beats per measure and the type of note that receives the beat. The top and bottom numbers convey these pieces of information.

Figure 3.6

The top number denotes how many beats there are per measure.

The bottom number denotes which type of note (value) serves as the beat (16 = sixteenth, 8 = eighth, 4 = quarter, 2 = half, 1 = whole).

BONUS

The time signature in Figure 3.6 is in simple meter, as the top number is 4. Due to this fact, the top number denotes the number of beats in each measure, four; the bottom number signifies the type of note value that represents the beat: the quarter note. The time signature is, therefore, communicating that there are four beats in each measure and that the quarter note is the note value that represents the beat. This does not mean that each measure can only have four quarter notes, but rather that each measure must have the equivalent note value of four quarter notes (see Figure 3.7).

Find the lyrics to one of your favorite songs. Count out the number of accented syllables in each line. Now do the same for a poem of your choice (Shakespeare and Emily Dickinson are excellent choices). Compare the meter of the poem to the meter of the song. What do you discover?

Figure 3.7

Parentheses are used to indicate beats that occur while a note is being held.

If the bottom number changes, then the note value that represents the beat also changes. For example, suppose we have the time signature $\frac{2}{8}$. We can immediately identify the type of meter: simple, as the top number is 2. Since the time signature represents simple meter, the top number denotes the number of beats per measure, two, and the bottom number denotes the type of note value that serves as the beat, the eighth note. Each measure of $\frac{2}{8}$ will contain two eighth notes, or the equivalent note value.

Duple, Triple, and Quadruple

Remember, any meter in which the beat can be divided by two is called simple meter, but there are several terms that combine with simple meter to discuss the number of beats per measure: duple, triple, and quadruple.

Duple

Duple meter is a type of simple meter characterized by a group of two beats per measure. The following meters are examples of duple. As the meter type is simple in both examples, they would be called simple duple.

In $\frac{2}{4}$ meter, each measure contains the note value of two quarter notes.

Figure 3.8

In $\frac{2}{4}$ meter, the notes may vary in value, but every measure will be equal to two beats (quarter notes).

Figure 3.9

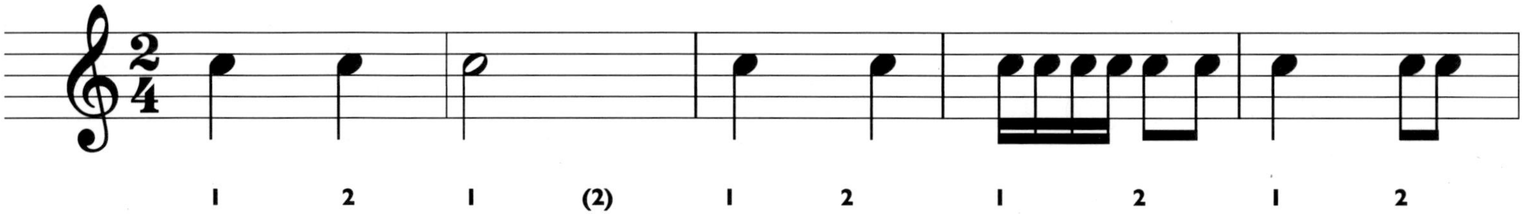

In $\frac{2}{2}$ meter, each measure contains the note value of two half notes. Again, the notes may vary in value, but each measure must be equal to two half notes.

Figure 3.10

Both examples ($\frac{2}{4}$ and $\frac{2}{2}$) contain two beats per measure, which makes them both duple meter. The difference between them, however, lies in the note value that gets the beat (the bottom number in the time signature).

Triple

Another type of simple meter is **triple meter**. In triple meter, each measure contains three beats. As the meter type is simple in both examples below, it would be called simple triple.

In $\frac{3}{2}$ meter, each measure contains the note value of three half notes.

Figure 3.11

In $\frac{3}{4}$ meter, each measure contains the note value of three quarter notes.

Figure 3.12

Both of the simple triple meter examples in Figures 3.11 and 3.12 contain three beats in each measure, which makes them both triple meter. The difference between these three meters lies in the note value that gets the beat (the bottom number).

Quadruple

In **quadruple meter,** there are four beats per measure. Again, since each of these beats is divisible by two, this is a form of simple meter called simple quadruple.

In $\frac{4}{2}$ meter, each measure contains the note value of four half notes.

Figure 3.13

In $\frac{4}{4}$ meter, each measure contains the note value of four quarter notes.

Figure 3.14

Activity 3.2—In-class activity

Fill in each measure below with notes that correspond to the requested time signature. Be creative with combinations of note values that fit each time signature.

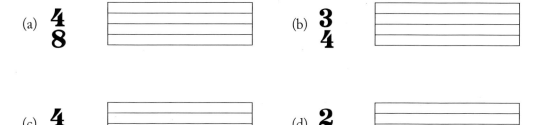

(a) **4/8**

(b) **3/4**

(c) **4/2**

(d) **2/4**

Beams in Simple Meter

A **beam** is a horizontal line, used in place of flags, that connects groups of notes together to represent a single beat. Beams help the performer read the music.

Figure 3.15 below is an example of two eighth notes beamed together in order to communicate one beat in the time signature **4/4**.

Figure 3.15

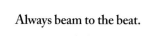

BONUS

Always beam to the beat.

The example below is a group of eighth notes in the time signature **3/4** not beamed together. This example is harder for the musician to read.

Figure 3.16

The proper way to beam in $\frac{3}{4}$ is shown below. Notice how the eighth notes are beamed in groups that represent a single beat. This makes it easier for someone reading the music because they see the eighth notes grouped together for each beat.

Figure 3.17

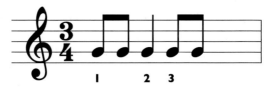

Counting Note Values in Simple Meter

In addition to understanding how time signatures that represent simple meter work, you must know how to express the rhythms when confronted with them. One way to do this is through a counting system. The counting system discussed in this book uses a number and a few different syllables to express the rhythmic ideas.

Counting the Beat

A number is used to express the beat in a measure. The meter in Figure 3.18 is simple, as the top number is 4, which means it has four beats in each measure. Furthermore, the quarter note receives the beat value. We use a number to represent each of the beats in each measure. Since there are four quarter notes in each measure, we will use the numbers 1, 2, 3, and 4 to express each beat.

Figure 3.18

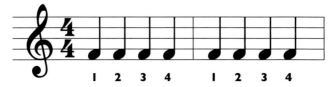

Regardless of time signature, a number represents the beat; Figure 3.19 illustrates this. Since the time signature of $\frac{2}{2}$ represents simple meter, we know that there are two beats in each measure (top number) and that the half note expresses the beat value (bottom number). This means that the beat is the half note, and we will use the numbers 1 and 2 to express the half-note beat.

Figure 3.19

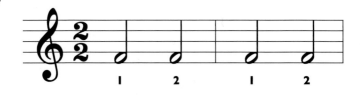

Counting the Subdivision of the Beat

For the subdivision of the beat, we use the syllable "and." Figure 3.20 is in $\frac{4}{4}$, meaning that there are four beats and that the quarter note receives the beat. In this meter, the subdivision of the beat is the eighth note. The quarter note beat still receives the numbers 1, 2, 3, and 4, but the subdivision, the eighth notes, gets the syllable "and."

Figure 3.20

Again, we use the syllable "and" to represent the subdivision of the beat in all types of simple meter. The meter in Figure 3.21 is simple. The beat value is therefore the half note (bottom number) and there are two beats in each measure (top number). The half note still receives the number, but the quarter note, as the subdivision, gets the syllable "and."

Figure 3.21

Counting Durations smaller than the Subdivision

If we want to express small rhythmic values—more divisions than the subdivision of the beat—we use the syllables "e" and "a." Going back to our example in $\frac{4}{4}$, we see that the beat is the quarter note and the eighth note is the subdivision. If we divide the subdivision into smaller units, we get the sixteenth notes as pictured in Figure 3.22. The second sixteenth note receives the syllable "e" and the fourth one receives the syllable "a."

Figure 3.22

In $\frac{2}{2}$, the beat is the half note, the subdivision is the quarter note, and the division greater than the subdivision is the eighth note. Figure 3.23 illustrates this concept.

Figure 3.23

We can have any different combinations of note values. Examine the figures below to see how different combinations change the counting system.

Figure 3.24

Figure 3.25

Activity 3.3—In-class activity

Using numbers, the syllables "&," "e," and "a," write in the counting for the exercises below. Make sure you know which note value gets the beat.

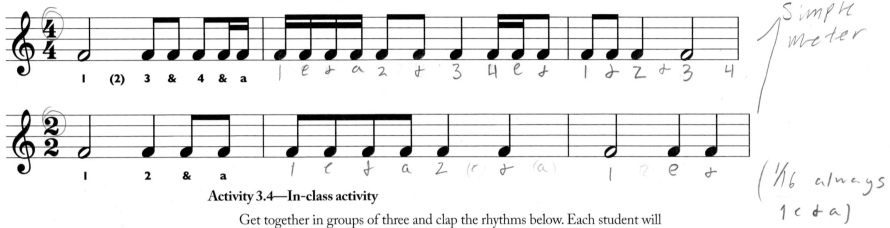

Activity 3.4—In-class activity

Get together in groups of three and clap the rhythms below. Each student will practice clapping his or her line individually. Once everyone understands their lines of rhythm, all three students will clap their lines simultaneously with each other. This may be hard at first, but practice it until you are able to clap your line while the other two students are clapping their lines. Write in the counting for each line.

First Student

Second Student

Third Student

Chapter 3 Review

ACROSS

3 Meter in which the beat is divided into two equal parts

6 A vertical stack of numbers that indicates meter

7 A horizontal bar that connects a group of notes into a single beat

8 A type of simple meter that is characterized by four beats per measure

9 The passage of pitch through time

10 A singular grouping of beats

DOWN

1 Meter that indicates the beat divides into three equal parts

2 A vertical line dividing measures on the staff

4 A repeated combination of the same number of beats in a piece

5 The fixed, rhythmic pulse of a piece of music

Daily Exercises for Chapter 3

❧ EXERCISES FOR DAY 1

Exercise 3.1

Read through chapter 3 and answer the following questions:

a) What is a beat?

b) What is meter?

c) What is a bar line?

d) What is a measure?

e) What is a time signature?

Exercise 3.2

What type of meter (simple or compound) do the time signatures below represent?

(a) $\frac{6}{8}$ *Compound*

(b) $\frac{4}{4}$ *Simple*

(c) $\frac{2}{8}$ *Simple*

(d) $\frac{9}{16}$ *Compound*

(e) $\frac{12}{4}$ *Compound*

(f) $\frac{3}{4}$ *Compound*

❧ EXERCISES FOR DAY 2

Exercise 3.3

What does the top number of a time signature that represents simple meter communicate?

What does the bottom number of a time signature that represents simple meter communicate?

Exercise 3.4

Complete the following using the excerpt below.

a) Using the appropriate numbers or syllables, write out the correct rhythm for the notes on the treble clef lines. The first measure has been done for you as an example.

b) Practice reading rhythm by counting or clapping the treble clef melody aloud.

When I Survey the Wondrous Cross

LENT

Words: Isaac Watts, 1707.
Music: 'Hamburg', Lowell Mason, 1824. Setting: "Northfield Hymnal", 1904.
copyright: public domain. This score is a part of the Open Hymnal Project, 2014 Revision.

BONUS

Remember: Always
beam to the beat.

𝄞 EXERCISES FOR DAY 3

Exercise 3.5

Fill in the correct note values to complete the following measures so that they match
the time signature. Be creative with combinations of notes that fit each time signature.

Exercise 3.6

On the staves provided, rewrite the given measures so that the notes are beamed correctly. Remember, beam to the beat.

Exercise 3.7

Identify the following time signatures as duple, triple, or quadruple.

(a) $\mathbf{\frac{2}{2}}$ _____

(b) $\mathbf{\frac{3}{4}}$ _____

(c) $\mathbf{\frac{4}{8}}$ _____

(d) $\mathbf{\frac{2}{16}}$ _____

(e) $\mathbf{\frac{4}{4}}$ _____

✿ EXERCISES FOR DAY 4

Exercise 3.8

Using numbers and the syllables "e," "&," and "a," count the exercises below. Make sure you know which note value gets the beat.

Exercise 3.9

Answer the following questions about the excerpt from "When Peace Like a River."
The second musical line is given for extra practice.

a) Starting with the first *full* measure (beginning on the word "peace"), write out the rhythm of the top notes in the treble clef (the melody). The first note is shown as an example.

b) Practice reading rhythm by counting or clapping the treble clef melody aloud.

c) Label the name of each note (e.g., A, B, C, etc.) on this excerpt to the right of the note.

4 Compound Meter

In chapter 3, we learned about different types of simple meters. Remember, these meters are called simple because their beats can be divided evenly into two parts. In this chapter, we will focus on compound meter, in which the beat is divided into three parts. Get ready to do some basic math as we learn about compound meter. Every time signature within compound meter must be translated in order to understand which type of note gets the beat and which type of note divides the beat into three parts.

Simple Meter vs. Compound Meter

Recall from chapter 3 that simple meter is defined as a meter in which each beat in a measure can be divided into two equal parts. Furthermore, when simple meter is translated into a time signature, the top number represents the number of beats in each measure and the bottom number represents the type of note value that receives the beat. We can identify the $\frac{2}{2}$ time signature in Figure 4.1 on the next page as simple meter because the top number is 2. The top number represents the number of beats in each measure, two, while the bottom number represents the note value that receives the beat, the half note.

Compound meter is defined as a meter in which the beat is divided into three equal parts. The time signatures that represent compound meter differ from those that represent simple meter because they do not give any indication of the beat or beat value; rather, they depict the subdivisions of the beat. The $\frac{6}{8}$ time signature in Figure 4.1 on the next page, which expresses compound meter, does not have six beats per measure, but rather has six subdivisions. The eighth note does not get the beat, but instead receives the subdivision of the beat.

When the morning stars sang together, and all the sons of God shouted for joy?

—Job 38:7 (KJV)

Figure 4.1

	simple meter	compound meter	
Number of beats per measure	**2**	**6**	number of **subdivisions** of the beat per measure
Note value that receives the beat	**2**	**8**	note value that receives the **subdivision** of the beat

Understanding Time Signatures in Compound Meter

Consider the $\frac{6}{8}$ time signature in the figure above. The top number is 6 and the bottom number is 8. Recall from chapter 3 that whenever the top number of a time signature is 6, 9, or 12, the meter is compound, so the meter represented by this time signature, called six-eight, is compound. Furthermore, the top number shows how many subdivisions of the beat are in each measure. In our example of $\frac{6}{8}$, the 6 tells us that each measure has a total of six subdivisions of the beat.

In compound meter, the bottom number of the time signature represents the note value of each subdivision of the beat. The 8 in the $\frac{6}{8}$ time signature tells us that the note value of one subdivision of the beat is the eighth note.

In summary, this time signature gives us three important pieces of information:

1. The meter it represents is compound.

2. There are six subdivisions of the beat in each measure.

3. The eighth note receives the subdivision.

As you may have realized, this time signature does not give us any information about the beat itself. But wait! Do you see clues about the beat value in the three bits of information that we do have? Think about the definition of compound meter. It's a meter in which each beat is subdivided into three parts. We know that in our example of $\frac{6}{8}$ time, the eighth note receives the subdivision. By multiplying the note that receives the subdivision of the beat by three, we find the value of the beat. In other words, the beat is divided into three eighth notes, so three eighth notes make up one beat. Three eighth notes are equal to the value of one dotted quarter note, so now we know that the dotted quarter note gets the beat in $\frac{6}{8}$ time!

Figure 4.2

$$\frac{6}{8} = ♪♪♪♪ = ♩.$$

BONUS

The beat value for all time signatures that express compound meter will be dotted. While their note value will change, as we will see later, the beat will always be dotted. A dotted note value is the only one that can contain three notes of equal value.

After you have found the beat value, you should be able to figure out the number of beats per measure. In our six-eight example, there are six subdivisions per measure, or six eighth notes. If we know that one beat is made up of three eighth notes, how many beats do six eighth notes make? Six divided by three is two. Six eighth notes make up two beats, so there are two beats per measure in six-eight time. Do you feel like you're in math class again? Good! Rhythm and meter are very mathematical! Figure 4.3 below gives a visual representation of the concepts discussed.

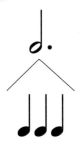

Figure 4.3

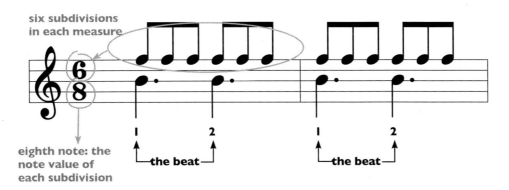

More Compound Time Signatures

As we've seen in compound time signatures, we can find the exact subdivision of the beat by looking at the bottom number in the time signature. For example, in six-eight time, the 8 on the bottom means the subdivisions are eighth notes, and therefore the beat is a dotted quarter note (the duration of three eighth notes).

BONUS

The beat value in compound meter will always be a dotted note.

To find the number of beats per measure in compound meter, divide the top number by three.

TIP: To count subdivisions of the beat in compound meter, use the syllables "1""&""a" "2""&""a" and so on.

Compound time signatures may have other numbers besides 8 on the bottom. Figure 4.4 shows a time signature of $\frac{9}{16}$. The 16 on the bottom means the sixteenth note is the subdivision. That means the beat is the dotted eighth note (the duration of three sixteenth notes). The 9 on the top means there are three beats per measure (remember the tip—divide the top number by three to find the number of beats).

Figure 4.4

Compound time signatures with a 4 at the bottom (Figure 4.5) indicate that the subdivisions are quarter notes and the beat is a dotted half note (the duration of three quarter notes). The 12 on top means there are four beats per measure (12 divided by 3).

Figure 4.5

Activity 4.1—In-class activity

Give the number of beats in each measure for the following compound meters:

(1) _____ $\frac{6}{4}$ (2) _____ $\frac{9}{8}$ (3) _____ $\frac{9}{4}$ (4) _____ $\frac{12}{8}$

(5) _____ $\frac{9}{16}$ (6) _____ $\frac{6}{8}$ (7) _____ $\frac{12}{16}$ (8) _____ $\frac{6}{16}$

Activity 4.2—In-class activity

How many beats per measure does this tune have? The song has two beats per measure with the dotted quarter note getting the beat. As you sing, what words to you tend to emphasize? Circle the words or syllables that you emphasize. Circle the notes that occur on the beats. You should find that the emphasis is on the beats of the song.

BONUS

Row, Row, Row Your Boat

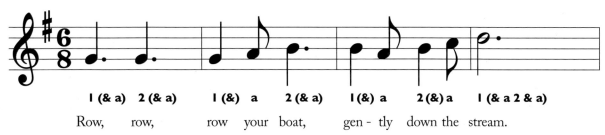

The sharp (♯) next to the clef is called a key signature. We will discuss key signatures in chapter 6.

Compound Duple, Triple, and Quadruple Meter

The definitions that we learned in chapter 3 for duple, triple, and quadruple meter remain the same:

Duple meter is a meter characterized by a grouping of two beats per measure.

Triple meter is a meter characterized by a grouping of three beats per measure.

Quadruple meter is a meter characterized by a grouping of four beats per measure.

Remember, in compound meter, the time signature doesn't readily give you the note value of the beat and the number of beats in each measure as it does in simple meter. You have to do the math first to find the beat in compound meter.

Like simple meter, compound meter can be described as duple, triple, or quadruple meter. Take a look at the chart below.

Top Number of Time Signature	Number of Beats per Measure	Type of Compound Meter
6	2	Duple
9	3	Triple
12	4	Quadruple

As this chart notates, when the top number is 6, the meter is duple, when it is 9, the meter is triple, and when it is 12, the meter is quadruple. Figure 4.6 illustrates duple, triple, and quadruple meter.

Figure 4.6

Compound Meter and Beaming

You may have noticed in the previous examples that, as in simple meter, notes in compound meter are also beamed together to help the performer read the music. Notes in both simple and compound meter are beamed together in groups that represent a single beat. In simple meter, two notes are beamed together. In compound meter, where the beat is subdivided into three, three notes are beamed together over one beat.

For example, the beams of a $\frac{6}{8}$ time signature are done in order to reveal the length of a full beat. The musician sees the two groups of eighth notes, and counts two beats.

Figure 4.7

Compare the two examples in Figure 4.8 below. In which example is it easier to see how the beats are grouped?

Figure 4.8

Beaming helps us see where the beats fall.

BONUS

Remember: Always beam to the beat.

Chapter 4 Review

_____ 1. Compound meter

_____ 2. Dotted notes

_____ 3. Compound triple meter

_____ 4. Compound quadruple meter

_____ 5. Top number in compound meter

_____ 6. Bottom number in compound meter

_____ 7. Compound duple meter

_____ 8. Dotted quarter note

_____ 9. Dotted half note

a) The note value of the subdivisions of the beat

b) The note that gets the beat in $\frac{9}{4}$ compound meter

c) Three beats per measure

d) With this meter, the beat is always on a dotted note

e) Four beats per measure

f) Only these notes can be divided into three equal parts

g) The number of subdivisions of the beat in each measure

h) The note that gets the beat in $\frac{6}{8}$ compound meter

i) Two beats per measure

Daily Exercises

🎶 EXERCISES FOR DAY 1

Exercise 4.1

Read through chapter 4 and answer the following questions:

1) How many subdivisions are in a beat of compound meter? *3*

2) In compound time signatures, what does the top number mean? *number of subdivision of the beat Per measure*

3) In compound time signatures, what does the bottom number mean? *note value that receives the subdivision of the beat*

4) In compound meter, how many beats do duple, triple, and quadruple meters have per measure? *1/2   1/3   1/4*

Exercise 4.2

Fill in each measure below with notes that correspond to the requested time signature. Be creative with combinations of note values that fit each time signature.

(a) **6/8** 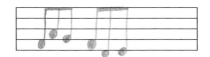   (b) **6/4**

(c) **6/16**    (d) **9/8**

Exercise 4.3

Write the note value of the beat in each of the following compound time signatures:

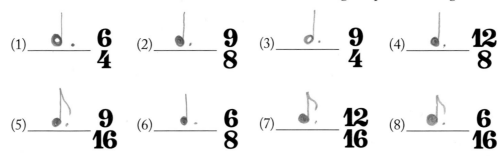

(1)_____ **6/4**   (2)_____ **9/8**   (3)_____ **9/4**   (4)_____ **12/8**

(5)_____ **9/16**   (6)_____ **6/8**   (7)_____ **12/16**   (8)_____ **6/16**

EXERCISES FOR DAY 2

Exercise 4.4

The following excerpt is the first line from Bach's "Jesu, Joy of Man's Desiring." Use this excerpt to answer the questions below. You may want to find a recording online in order to listen to the piece and study the rhythm.

1) How many beats are in each measure? 3

2) Which note value is getting the beat? dotted 1/4 note ♩.

3) Are the eighth notes in the treble clef beamed correctly? yes

4) Why or why not? cuz, beamed to the beat

Exercise 4.5

Match the simple and compound time signatures with the correct criteria (there may
be more than one answer for each time signature).

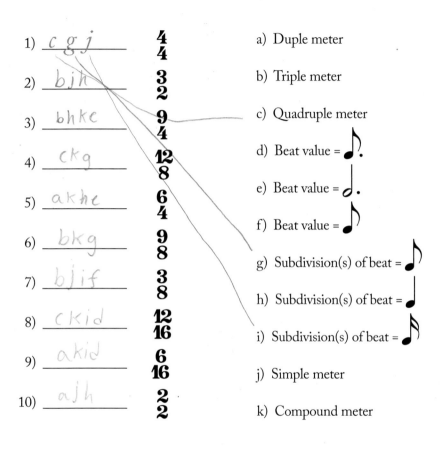

1) _c g j_ $\frac{4}{4}$ a) Duple meter

2) _b j h_ $\frac{3}{2}$ b) Triple meter

3) _b h k e_ $\frac{9}{4}$ c) Quadruple meter

4) _c k g_ $\frac{12}{8}$ d) Beat value = ♪.

5) _a k h e_ $\frac{6}{4}$ e) Beat value = 𝅗𝅥.

6) _b k g_ $\frac{9}{8}$ f) Beat value = ♪

7) _b j i f_ $\frac{3}{8}$ g) Subdivision(s) of beat = ♪

8) _c k i d_ $\frac{12}{16}$ h) Subdivision(s) of beat = ♩

9) _a k i d_ $\frac{6}{16}$ i) Subdivision(s) of beat = ♪

10) _a j h_ $\frac{2}{2}$ j) Simple meter

                                             k) Compound meter

*...Thus much of music,
which makes a fair ending;
for what should be the end
of music if not the love of
beauty?*

—Plato

❦ EXERCISES FOR DAY 3

Exercise 4.6

Rewrite the following examples so that the notes are beamed correctly. Remember, beam notes to the beat.

EXERCISES FOR DAY 4

Exercise 4.7

Match the correct time signature with the melodies below.

a) **6/4**   b) **9/8**   c) **3/8**   d) **6/8**   e) **4/4**

1. _____ b _____

2. _____ c _____

3. _____ a _____

4. _____ e _____

5. _____ d _____

Exercise 4.8

Given the time signatures below, identify the meter type, the number of beats in each measure, and the note value that receives the beat.

	Meter type	Beats/ measure	Note value
(a) **6/8**	C	2	♩
(b) **4/4**	S	4	♩.
(c) **9/16**	C	3	♪.
(d) **12/16**	C	4	♪.
(e) **3/2**	S	3	𝅝
(f) **2/8**	S	2	♪
(g) **12/4**	C	4	♩.

5 Scales

In this chapter, you will learn about the major and natural minor scales and their patterns of whole steps and half steps. Understanding scales is one of the most fundamental requirements for music theory and performance. Scales are the building blocks for creating most music.

Recognizing scale patterns in music will help you read music more quickly and prepare you for more complex music theory concepts.

A **scale** is a series of musical notes organized by ascending or descending pitches. These pitches begin with the **tonic**, which is the most important note of the scale and gives the scale its name. All other notes will point the listener back to the tonic.

What is a Major Scale?

Major scales begin and end with the same note (the tonic note) and each letter name in between is presented only once (one A, one B, one C, etc.). As we learned in chapter 1, the space between the first and last notes, since they are the same pitch and letter name, is called an octave. A **major scale** is a series of eight notes that begins and ends with the same note, an octave apart, and follows this pattern of whole steps (W) and half steps (H) in ascending order: W–W–H–W–W–W–H. You will need to memorize this pattern of whole steps and half steps for the major scale.

BONUS

The C major scale is the only major scale without any flats or sharps, so it contains only white keys.

Figure 5.1

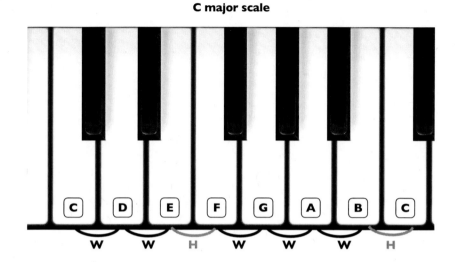

C major scale

If needed, go back to chapter 1 to review the difference between whole steps and half steps.

For example, the C major scale is the pattern of whole steps and half steps for the major scale whose tonic note is C. If the scale is descending, the pattern works backward: H–W–W–W–H–W–W. This pattern remains the same no matter what the tonic and root note. In other words, no matter what note we begin with, the pattern of W-W-H-W-W-W-H remains the same for every ascending major scale.

Since the sequence of W–W–H–W–W–W–H serves as a pattern for all major scales, it can be applied to any starting note. For example, by starting on G and applying the pattern of whole steps and half steps ascending, it creates the scale found in Figure 5.2.

Figure 5.2

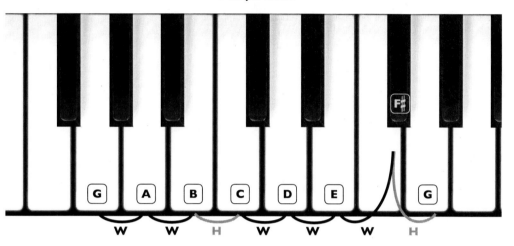

G major scale

By following the major scale pattern of whole steps and half steps, you will find that the G major scale consists of one sharp (F♯). Again, the pattern W–W–H–W–W–W–H can be started on any note and the scale it creates will be a major scale.

Activity 5.1—In-class activity

Using the paper keyboard in the Helpful Tools section, determine the exact notes of the following major scales using the major scale pattern of whole steps and half steps. Have one student start with the first note and then have another student give the next note of the scale in descending or ascending order. Continue this exercise between the students until the scale is completed with the eighth note.

a) **D** major scale <u>(D)</u> <u>E</u> <u>F#</u> <u>G</u> <u>A</u> <u>B</u> <u>C</u> <u>D</u>

remember: W   W   H   W   W   W   H

b) **A** major scale <u>A</u> <u>B</u> <u>C#</u> <u>D</u> <u>E</u> <u>F#</u> <u>G#</u> <u>A</u>

c) **E** major scale ___ ___ ___ ___ ___ ___ ___ ___

d) Choose a major scale and fill in the notes of that major scale:

___ ___ ___ ___ ___ ___ ___ ___

While it is important to recognize scales on your keyboard, it is also important to be able to notate scales (to **notate** means to write music on a staff). In Figure 5.3, the C major scale is notated on the treble and bass clefs in ascending and descending order.

Figure 5.3

Natural Minor Scales

Like major scales, natural minor scales begin and end with the same note (the tonic note), and each letter name in between is presented only once (one A, one B, one C, etc.). The natural minor scale consists of a different pattern of whole steps and half steps, and sounds different from a major scale. If you have access to a keyboard, compare the sound of a major scale (C-D-E-F-G-A-B-C) and a natural minor scale (A-B-C-D-E-F-G-A). Or, go online to find a website that will allow you to listen to these scales. The **natural minor scale** (Figure 5.4) is a series of eight notes containing this specific pattern of whole steps and half steps in ascending order: W–H–W–W–H–W–W. You will need to memorize this pattern of whole and half steps for the natural minor scale.

Figure 5.4

A natural minor scale

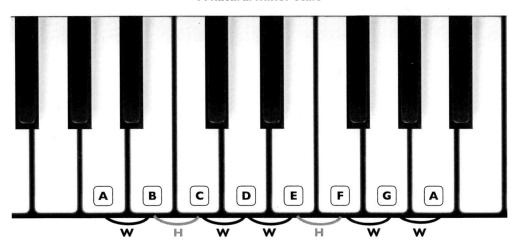

If the scale is descending, the pattern works backward: W–W–H–W–W–H–W.

By following the natural minor scale pattern of whole steps and half steps, you will find that the A natural minor is the only minor scale without any flats or sharps, so it contains only white keys.

In Figure 5.5, the A natural minor scale is notated on the treble and bass clefs, in ascending and descending order.

[handwritten margin notes: C Major 1121112; (F#) G Major 112112; Major 12112; Natural minor 121121]

Figure 5.5

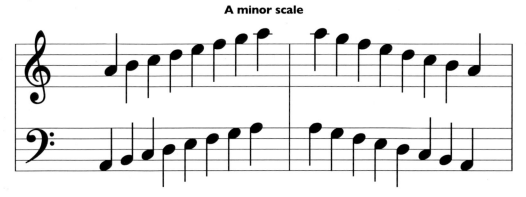

A minor scale

As was the case with the major scale pattern, the natural minor scale pattern can be started on any note. For example, starting on E and building a minor scale using the natural minor scale pattern of whole steps and half steps in ascending order creates:

Figure 5.6

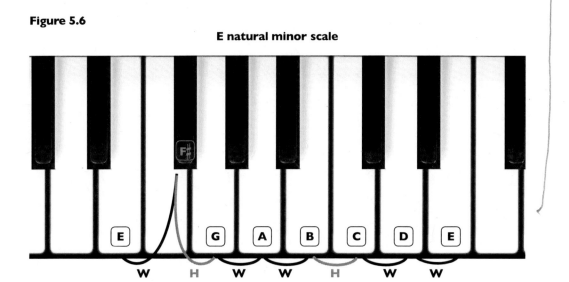

E natural minor scale

By following the natural minor scale pattern of whole steps and half steps, you find that the E natural minor scale consists of one sharp (F♯). This natural minor scale pattern of whole steps and half steps works with every natural minor scale that exists in our Western system.

There are also other patterns of whole and half steps for minor scales, but for the purposes of this text, we will focus only on natural minor scales. If you want to know more about these other patterns used to create additional types on minor scales, refer to the Supplemental Material section.

Relative Major and Minor Scales

One final thing to note about major and minor scales is their relationship to each other. You may have noticed that neither the C major scale in Figure 5.1 nor the A minor scale in Figure 5.4 had any sharps or flats. They are related in this way. The A minor scale is the relative minor to C major.

Figure 5.7

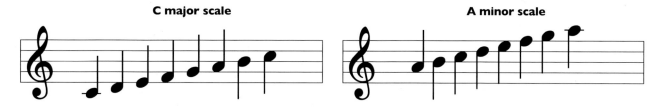

Every major scale has a **relative minor scale** associated with it. In other words, for every major scale, there is a minor scale that uses the same sharps and flats. A quick way to find the relative minor is to start on the sixth note of the major scale, and build the minor scale up, using the same sharps and flats that the major scale used. For example, in the C major scale above, which has no sharps or flats, the sixth note is A. When we build our scale beginning on A, with no sharps or flats, we create A minor, which is the relative minor to C major.

Figure 5.8 shows a few more examples of major scales and their corresponding natural minor scales. Notice that the minor scales have the same number of flats and sharps as the major scales to their left. On the Internet, locate and listen to an audio example of each of these scales.

Figure 5.8

Chapters 1–5 Review

_____ g _____   1. ACEG

_____ j _____   2. Augmentation dot

_____ l _____   3. Beat

_____ r _____   4. Bottom number in simple meter

_____ o _____   5. Compound meter

_____ u _____   6. D-E-F♯-G-A-B-C♯-D

_____ v _____   7. D-E-F-G-A-B♭-C-D

_____ d _____   8. EGBDF

_____ c _____   9. Enharmonic equivalent

_____ c _____   10. FACE

_____ f _____   11. GBDFA

_____ a _____   12. Half step

_____ m _____   13. Meter

_____ i _____   14. Quarter note

_____ n _____   15. Simple meter

_____ k _____   16. Tie

_____ p _____   17. Time signature

_____ q _____   18. Top number in simple meter

_____ h _____   19. Whole note

_____ b _____   20. Whole step

_____ t _____   21. W-H-W-W-H-W-W

_____ s _____   22. W-W-H-W-W-W-H

a. The shortest distance between two notes

b. The distance of pitch equal to two half steps

c. Two notes that have the same pitch but different names

d. Notation on the staff lines in a treble clef

e. Notation in the spaces of the staff in a treble clef

f. Notation on the staff lines in a bass clef

g. Notation in the spaces of the staff in a bass clef

h. Twice the value of a half note

i. Twice the value of an eighth note

j. Increases the note value of a note or rest by half the value of the note or rest

k. Used to add the lengths of two notes together to prolong the pitch

l. The fixed, rhythmic pulse of a piece of music

m. The specific beat groupings and divisions that occur within the music

n. Meter in which the beat is divided into two equal parts

o. Meter in which the beat is divided into three equal parts

p. A vertical stack of numbers placed at the beginning of the staff immediately following the clef to indicate the meter

q. Denotes how many beats there are per measure

r. Denotes which type of note serves as the beat

s. The pattern of whole and half steps in a major scale

t. The pattern of whole and half steps in a natural minor scale

u. D major scale

v. D minor scale

Daily Exercises for Chapter 5

🎼 EXERCISES FOR DAY 1

Exercise 5.1

Read through chapter 5 and answer the following questions:

a) What is a scale?

a series of notes organized by ascending or descending pitches

b) If both the major and minor scales contain eight notes, what is the difference between major and minor scales?

the whole and half step patterns

c) What is the pattern of whole steps and half steps for major scales?

w w H w w w H

d) What is the pattern of whole steps and half steps for natural minor scales?

w H w w H w w

e) What is the term for the distance between two notes with the same name?

octive

Exercise 5.2

Practice recognizing whole steps and half steps on a staff by labeling the following distances between the pairs of notes in each measure as either a whole step or a half step.

1.

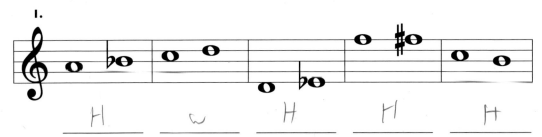

H   w   H   H   H

2. Write your own pairs of notes with the indicated half step or whole step. Use sharps and flats, if needed.

whole step   half step   whole step   whole step   half step

Exercise 5.3

Fill in the missing notes to the scales given below by notating them on the staff.

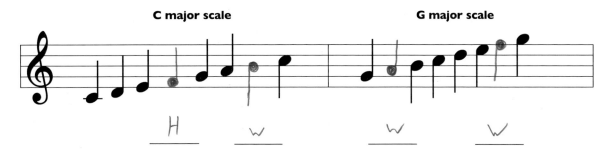

Label each note you just notated as either a whole or half step from the note before it.

✵ EXERCISES FOR DAY 2

Exercise 5.4

Fill in the missing notes in the following major scales. Use the keyboard sheet in the Helpful Tools section if you need to.

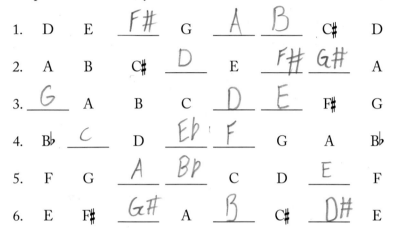

1. D   E   F#   G   A   B   C#   D

2. A   B   C#   D   E   F#   G#   A

3. G   A   B   C   D   E   F#   G

4. Bb   C   D   Eb   F   G   A   Bb

5. F   G   A   Bb   C   D   E   F

6. E   F#   G#   A   B   C#   D#   E

Take two scales from above and notate the scales on the staves below. Notate the scales in ascending and descending order, with one scale in the treble clef and one in the bass clef. If there are sharps or flats, place them to the left of the note.

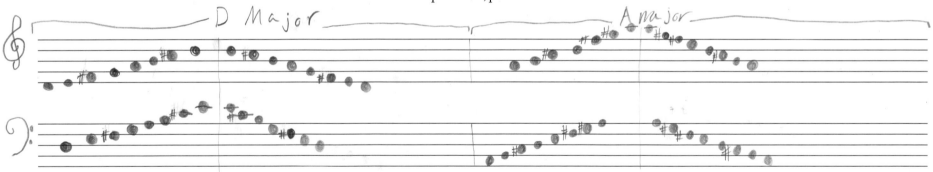

D Major   A Major

Exercise 5.5

Use the major and minor scale patterns of whole steps and half steps to answer
the questions below. You may find it helpful to use the keyboard sheet in the Helpful
Tools section.

a) How many sharps are in the D major scale? *2*

b) How many flats are in the E♭ major scale? *3*

c) How many flats are in the C natural minor scale? *3*

d) How many sharps are in the F♯ natural minor scale? *3*

EXERCISES FOR DAY 3

Exercise 5.6

In each example, the first note of the scale is given. Notate the indicated ascending
and descending major scale. Use sharps and flats to the left of the note if needed.
Note: Once a sharp or a flat appears, it is assumed that it applies through the end of
the measure unless notated otherwise.

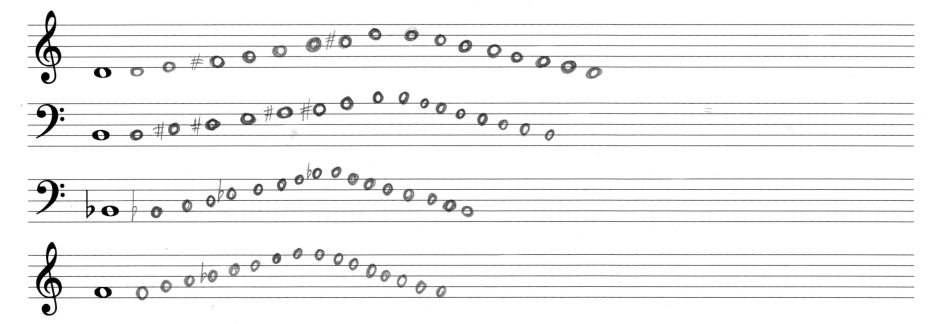

Exercise 5.7

In each example, the first note of the scale is given. Notate the indicated ascending and descending natural minor scale. Use sharps and flats to the left of the note if needed.

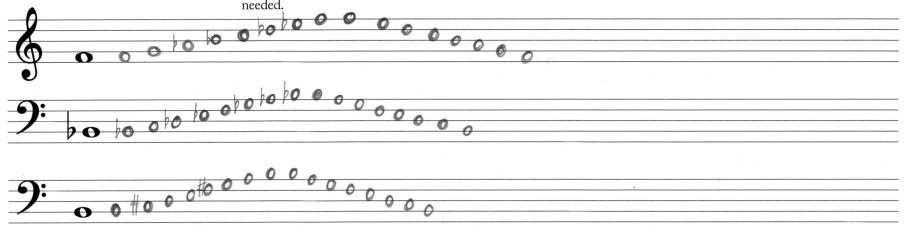

🎼 EXERCISES FOR DAY 4

Exercise 5.8

a) Write a melody in the following blank measures using only the notes that are part of the E major scale. You will need to add sharps or flats to specific notes.

b) Write a melody in the following blank measures using only the notes that are part of the A♭ major scale. You will need to add sharps or flats to specific notes.

Exercise 5.9

Identify the following major or natural minor scales. Remember, descending scales use the pattern backwards. It might be helpful to label whole steps and half steps on the scale so you can identify major or minor correctly.

1. _B natural minor_   2. _E Major_

3. _A minor_   4. _G major_

5. _D natural minor_   6. _Bb major_

6 Key Signatures

In chapter 5, you learned about major and natural minor scales, which served as a general introduction to the concept of musical keys. With this basic introduction, it is time to move forward and study what keys are and how they are expressed.

When we speak of a musical key, we're not talking about the keys on the piano. A definition of a **musical key** is the specific set of pitches used to create a piece of music. But what does that mean? In simple terms, the "key" of a composition is the scale around which the piece of music is centered. A piece in the key of G major would be based on the G major scale, and the tonic, G, would be the most important note in the piece. When listening to a piece of music, this is the tone that provides listeners with a sense of rest, the feeling of "coming home."

Key Signatures

The **key signature** is the organization of flats and sharps shown at the beginning of the staff that indicates in which key the music is written. For example, in Figure 6.1 on the next page, the three flats at the beginning of the staff indicate that this piece is in the key of E♭ and is based on the E♭ major scale (E♭ F G A♭ B♭ C D E♭). Because of the key signature, unless otherwise indicated, every E in the piece is an E♭. Every A is an A♭, and every B is a B♭. The composer does not need to write the flat beside each note because the key signature at the beginning of the staff tells the performer which notes are flatted throughout the piece.

BONUS

The key signature highlighted at right represents the key of E♭ major.

Figure 6.1

Be   thou   my   vi - sion   O

These key signatures are established and derived from scales. Let's use the G major scale as an example. By using the patterns of half steps and whole steps discussed in chapter 5, we find out that a major scale built on G has one sharp: F♯. We extract all of the sharps in this scale, and place them at the beginning of the staff. In this case, there is only the F♯, so that is what is at the beginning of the staff.

Figure 6.2   G Major

In Western music there are fifteen different key signatures that represent thirty (fifteen major and fifteen minor) different keys. No key signatures include both sharps and flats. They contain either sharps or flats (or neither, as with C major and A minor). By using key signatures at the beginning of each staff, composers tell the reader which notes should be sharped or flatted throughout the piece so that they do not have to write them in front of every note.

Let's look at another example. The D major scale is written in Figure 6.3 with a key signature consisting of two sharps. In the scale below, notice that the sharps are not placed next to the notes, but instead are found within the key signature written at the beginning of the score. This denotes a sharp on the notes that should be sharped within D major: D-E-F♯-G-A-B-C♯-D.

Figure 6.3

[The Order of Sharps and Flats]

order of ♭

order of ♯

Flats or sharps always occur in a certain order in a key signature. The order of flats is B E A D G C F. Therefore, if a key has only one flat, it will be a B♭. If a key has two flats, they will be a B♭ and E♭, and so on. A helpful way to memorize the order of flats is with the mnemonic "Before Eating A Doughnut, Get Coffee First."

Sharps also appear in a certain order: F C G D A E B. Notice that the order of sharps is the opposite of the order of flats. Therefore, if a key includes one sharp, it will be F♯. If the key has two sharps, they will be F♯ and C♯, and so on. The order of sharps and flats must be memorized. A helpful way to memorize the order of sharps is with the mnemonic "Fried Chicken Goes Down After Every Bite."

Since you now know how a key signature denotes which notes are to be sharped and flatted throughout a score, look back on Figure 6.3 at the D major scale. The sharped notes in that key are F♯ and C♯, which are precisely the notes indicated by the key signature. For a representation of this on the keyboard, see Figure 6.4.

Figure 6.4

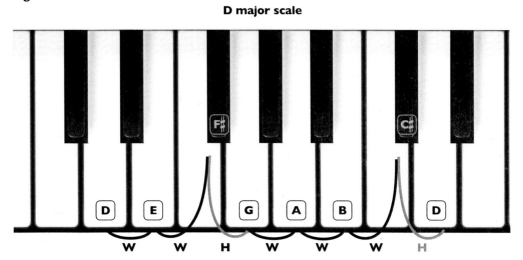

D major scale

BONUS

ORDER OF FLATS

Before Eating A Doughnut, Get Coffee First

ORDER OF SHARPS

Fried Chicken Goes Down After Every Bite

Music is a moral law. It gives a soul to the universe, wings to the mind, flight to the imagination, a charm to sadness, gaiety and life to everything. It is the essence of order, and leads to all that is good, just, and beautiful, of which it is the invisible, but nevertheless dazzling, passionate, and eternal form.

—Plato, as quoted by Sir John Lubbock

BONUS

An accidental that occurs within a measure applies only to the measure in which it occurs.

Before reading a piece of music, look at the key signature to understand in which key the piece is written and which notes will be sharped or flatted throughout. Just as a cook checks the list of ingredients in a recipe before preparing it, a musician checks the key signature to see which notes are included in a song before playing it.

Accidentals

As you learned in chapter 1, an accidental is a sharp (♯), flat (♭), or natural (♮) symbol placed to the left of a note. In the context of key signatures, the term accidental refers to the temporary alteration of a pitch.

Circle of Fifths

As you learned earlier in the chapter, there are thirty different key signatures (fifteen major, and fifteen minor). Although it is important that you know all of them, do not panic, because there are methods for helping you learn them more quickly. One of those methods is a diagram called the Circle of Fifths (see next page).

If you notice at the top of the chart in Figure 6.5, we have the key of C major. We know that there are no sharps or flats in the C major key, so we put a natural sign under the C.

Rotating clockwise, the progression of key signatures moves from the key of C major to the key with only one sharp (G major). G major then moves to the key with two sharps (D major) and the pattern continues on to A major (three sharps) and E major (four sharps), etc. The distance from C to G is five lines and spaces, known as a fifth. The distance from G to D is also a fifth (five lines and spaces). In fact, the distance between any two key signatures around the circle is a fifth. Thus we have the name "Circle of Fifths."

Rotating counterclockwise, the progression of key signatures moves from the key of C major to the key with only one flat (F major). F major then moves to the key with two flats (B♭ major) and the pattern continues on to E♭ major (three flats) and A♭ major (four flats) etc.

Activity 6.1—In-class activity

Refer to your Circle of Fifths chart to answer the following questions:

a) How many sharps does the key of E major have? __4__

b) How many flats does the key of A♭ major have? __4__

c) Which notes are flatted in the key of E♭ major? __3   A♭ B♭ E♭__

d) Which notes are sharped in the key of A major? __3   C♯ E♯ G♯__

Figure 6.5 The Circle of Fifths

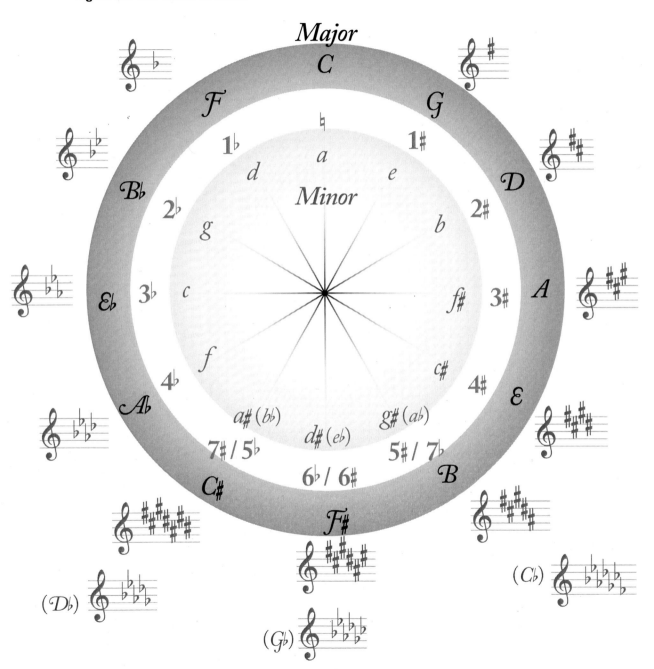

Writing Key Signatures

If you are writing the key signature of E major, you will find that you must write the key signature with four sharps, which must be in the correct order. In the same way, key signatures with flats must be written with the correct order of flats.

In Figure 6.6 you have an example of the order of sharps that appear in the key signature from left to right.

Figure 6.6

You can see how important it is to memorize the order of sharps and flats. You can tell quickly that in the key of A major, you will have three sharps in the following order: F♯–C♯–G♯.

Figure 6.7

In Figure 6.8 you have an example of the order of flats that appear in the key signature from left to right.

Figure 6.8

Again we see the importance of memorizing the order of sharps and flats so that you will know, for instance, that in the key of D♭ major, you will have five flats in the following order: B♭–E♭–A♭–D♭–G♭.

Figure 6.9

Key Signature Identification Methods

In addition to writing key signatures, there are a few methods to help you identify them. One, as discussed earlier, is the Circle of Fifths. Others are the "last sharp" and "second to last flat" methods. While these methods are extremely helpful, you should also work to memorize these key signatures as best you can. Beginning the memorization process now will assist you with more advanced concepts later.

Last Sharp Method

Look at the last sharp in a key signature consisting of sharps, and then move one half step higher. This will be the name of the key. In Figure 6.10, there are two sharps: F♯ and C♯. The last sharp is a C♯. A half step higher than C♯ is D. The key for the key signature pictured is D major.

Figure 6.10

Be cautious when using this method with a key signature of six or seven sharps. In Figure 6.11, the last sharp on the key signature is E♯. E♯ is also the enharmonic equivalent of F♮. What note is one half step higher than F♮? The answer is F♯. So our key signature is F♯ major (six sharps).

Figure 6.11

Second to Last Flat Method

In key signatures with flats, the second to last flat is always the tonic of the key signature and therefore the name of the key. In our example pictured on the left, what is the second to last flat representing? It is the E♭.

Therefore, our key signature is the key of E♭ major (three flats).

Relative Keys

In our quick study of major and natural minor scales, we have seen that every major scale has a natural minor scale associated with it, which uses the same flats or sharps as the major scale. Thus, every major key has a minor key associated with it. C major and A minor both have no sharps or flats in their scales. G major and E minor both have one sharp (F♯) in their scales.

These are **relative keys**, so called because they are pairs of major and minor scales that share the same key signature. C major is the relative major of A minor because both contain no sharps or flats. Or we could say that A minor is the relative minor to C major. Their key signatures are exactly the same.

Recall from chapter 5 that there is an easy way to determine which keys are relative to each other. Take the first note of the major scale (for example, the C major scale) and go up to the sixth note. A is the sixth note in the C major scale, so A minor is the relative minor key of C major.

Figure 6.12

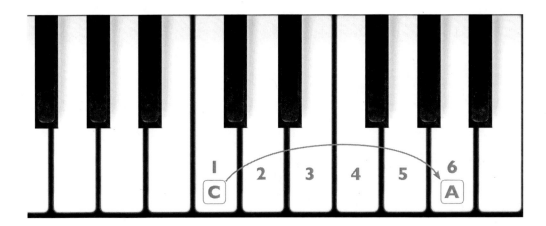

If you want to go from the minor key to the relative major, you take the first note of a minor key and then go up to the third note of the minor key. For example, look at the E minor scale. Using this concept for relative keys, you can determine its relative major scale. By starting the first note of E minor, we go up to the third note, G, and find that G major is the relative key to E minor.

Figure 6.13

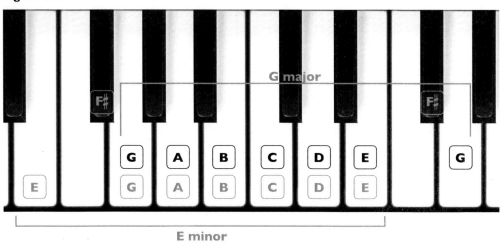

Looking back at our Circle of Fifths chart, notice the inner circle of the chart. In the inner circle, the lowercase letters are the relative minor keys.

Enharmonic Keys

On the Circle of Fifths diagram, you will notice that there are a few major key signatures with two different names. We have learned about enharmonic equivalent notes, but what about enharmonic equivalent key signatures? **Enharmonic equivalent key signatures** are two scales with the same sounding notes that can be called by two different names.

For example, F♯ major and G♭ major have the same-sounding notes in their scales because those two notes are enharmonically equivalent.

F♯ Major: F♯–G♯–A♯–B–C♯–D♯–E♯–F♯

G♭ Major: G♭–A♭–B♭–C♭–D♭–E♭–F–G♭

Figure 6.14

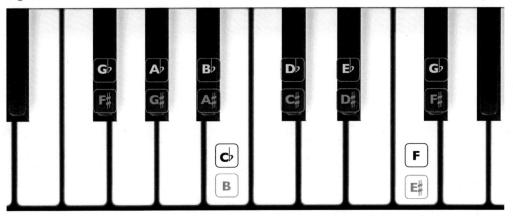

Why is this important? Many musicians and composers want to be consistent in playing with keys containing either flats or sharps. If a composer wanted to switch from the key of C♯ major (seven sharps) to the key of F♯ major (six sharps), it would be relatively easy since there is only one sharp difference between the keys. If the composer switched from C♯ major (seven sharps) to the key of G♭ major (six flats), it would be more confusing to read or play since the musician would need to translate the flats to sharps, even though G♭ major and F♯ major include the same-sounding notes. Consistent use of sharps or flats is one way that composers make it easier for musicians to read their music.

Chapter 6 Review

Some questions may have more than one answer.

_____j_____ 1. Indicates the key of the piece at the beginning of the staff by showing which sharps or flats are to be used

_____f_____ 2. Order of sharps that appears in key signatures from left to right

_____b_____ 3. Order of flats that appears in key signatures from left to right

_____k_____ 4. Pairs of major and minor scales that share the same key signature

_____e_____ 5. The key of F♯ major and G♭ major are said to be this

_____a,h_____ 6. Key signature with three sharps

_____c,i_____ 7. Key signature with five sharps

_____g,d_____ 8. Key signature with one flat

a. A major

b. B E A D G C F

c. B major

d. D minor

e. Enharmonic equivalent key signatures

f. F C G D A E B

g. F major

h. F♯ minor

i. G♯ minor

j. Key signature

k. Relative keys

Daily Exercises for Chapter 6

EXERCISES FOR DAY 1

Exercise 6.1

Read through chapter 6 and answer the following questions. Draw your own circle of fifths diagram on a piece of scrap paper for practice.

a) How many key signatures are in our Western style of music?   15

b) What is a musical key?   a set of pitches used to make a piece of music; the scale around which music is centered

c) In the Circle of Fifths diagram, starting on C major, which direction do the key signatures with sharps move? Which direction do the key signatures with flats move?

clockwise   counterclockwise

d) What are enharmonic keys? Give an example, including the notes in the keys.

2 scales by different names but sound the same

D flat major and c sharp major

✿ EXERCISES FOR DAY 2

Exercise 6.2

Practice drawing your own circle of fifths diagram on scrap paper.

On the staves below and on the next page, write the indicated major key signature. Be sure to provide the correct order of sharps or flats within the key signature.

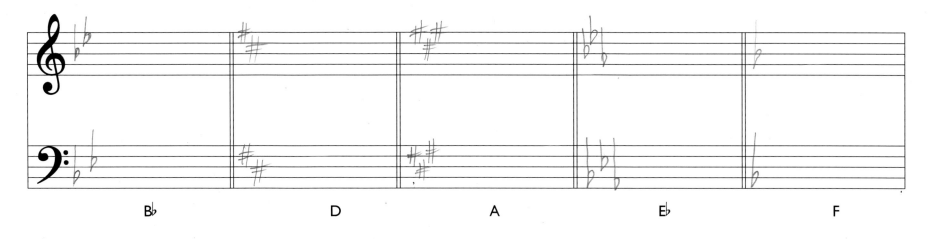

B♭   D   A   E♭   F

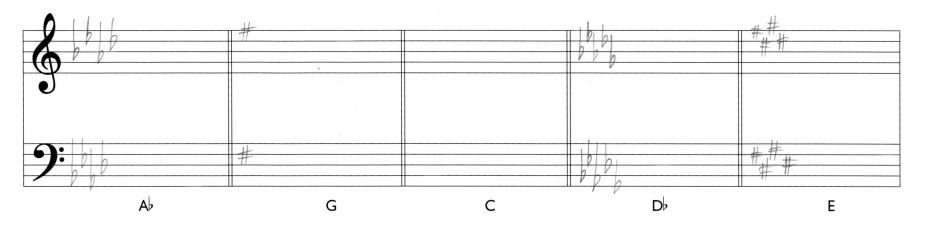

A♭   G   C   D♭   E

❧ EXERCISES FOR DAY 3

Exercise 6.3

Use the first line excerpt below from the hymn "Be Thou My Vision" to answer the questions below.

a) What major key is the piece above in? *Eb Major*

b) Which notes are flatted in the key signature above? *B, E, A*

c) Which note value gets the beat? How many beats are in each measure? *quarter note. 3 beats per measure*

d) Circle all the notes in the piece in both the treble and bass clefs that are flats (key signature will help). *✓*

e) In the second measure, treble clef, is there a whole step or half step step between the first two notes? *whole*

Exercise 6.4

Use the first line excerpt below from the hymn "When I Survey the Wondrous Cross" to answer the questions below.

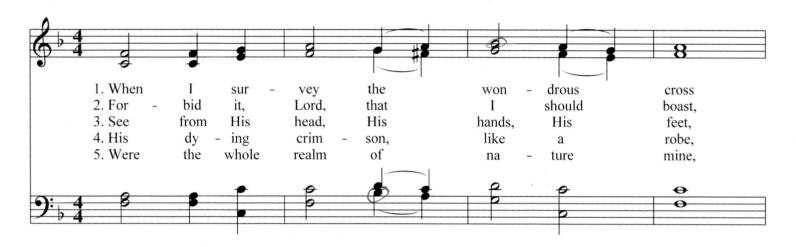

1. When   I   sur - vey   the   won - drous   cross
2. For - bid   it,   Lord,   that   I   should   boast,
3. See   from   His   head,   His   hands,   His   feet,
4. His   dy - ing   crim - son,   like   a   robe,
5. Were   the   whole   realm   of   na - ture   mine,

a) What major key is the excerpt above in?   F major

b) What are the notes of the scale in the key above?
        F, G, A, Bb, C, D, E, F

c) Circle all the notes in the piece in both the treble and bass clefs that are flats (key signature will help).

d) Which note in this first line is not in the key signature of the piece? How do you know it is not in the key?   F#. Key= F Major   no F# in key) because of
                                                                                                          #

e) Using the Circle of Fifths chart, which key going counterclockwise is after the key in this piece? How many flats or sharps are in this next key?
        Bb major 2bs

Exercise 6.5

Using the techniques discussed in chapter 6, match the relative keys.

1. __c__ D minor   a) B♭ major

2. __f__ C major   b) G major

3. __b__ E minor   c) F major

4. __c__ A major   d) B minor

5. __a__ G minor   e) F♯ minor

6. __D__ D major   f) A minor

🎼 EXERCISES FOR DAY 4

Exercise 6.6

On the staves below and on the next page, write the indicated minor key signature.
Be sure to provide the correct order of sharps or flats within the key signature. It may
be helpful to find the relative major key first in order to write the correct key signature
for each minor key.

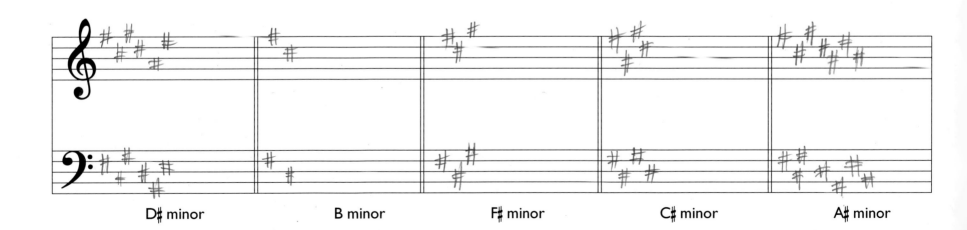

D♯ minor   B minor   F♯ minor   C♯ minor   A♯ minor

G♯ minor   A minor   E minor   E♭ minor   D minor

Exercise 6.7

Match the following key signatures to the correct key.

a) A minor   b) C♯ major   c) C minor   d) E major   e) D♭ major   f) C♭ major

g) D♯ minor   h) G♭ major   i) B minor   j) B major

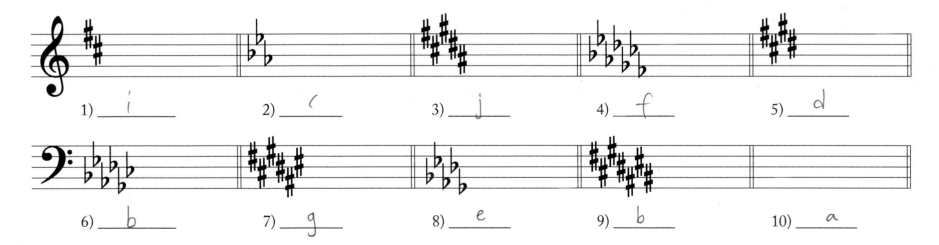

1) ___i___   2) ___f___   3) ___j___   4) ___f___   5) ___d___

6) ___b___   7) ___g___   8) ___e___   9) ___b___   10) ___a___

7 Scale Degrees and Transposition

In chapters 5 and 6 you learned about scales and key signatures. In this chapter you will expand upon your knowledge of scales by discussing scale degree numbers and names. Furthermore, you will put that knowledge into practice as we work to transpose melodies. The knowledge and skill you will learn in this chapter will not only be useful in your final project but also in understanding the relationship of notes in a scale.

Musical Degrees

Each note of the scale has a **scale degree**, which is simply the name or number of a note in a scale. Scale degree numbers are written with a little caret (∧) above the number. Look at the C (Figure 7.1) and D (Figure 7.2) major scales with the scale degree numbers written below them.

Figure 7.1 C major scale

Figure 7.2 D major scale

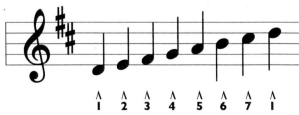

Most people use music as a couch; they want to be pillowed on it, relaxed and consoled for the stress of daily living. But serious music was never meant to be soporific.

—Aaron Copland

Examine the C major scale in Figure 7.1. Notice that the note C is the first degree of the scale, the note D is the second degree, the note E is the third, and so on until the scale ends one octave above the starting note C. The octave is given the number $\hat{1}$ because it is the same note as the first scale degree.

Scale Degree Names

A helpful way to understand scale degrees and their purpose is to use the scale degree names. Each scale degree number also has a scale degree name.

Scale Degree Number	Scale Degree Name	Meaning
$\hat{1}$	tonic	most important note; the tonal center
$\hat{2}$	supertonic	above ("super") the tonic
$\hat{3}$	mediant	middle note between tonic and dominant
$\hat{4}$	subdominant	below ("sub") the dominant
$\hat{5}$	dominant	second-most important note
$\hat{6}$	submediant	lower mediant (between subdominant and tonic)
$\hat{7}$	leading tone	strong pull ("leads") to the tonic
$\hat{1}$	tonic	upper tonic—the tonal center, an octave higher

The **tonic** is the first and most important degree in a scale. In Western music, most of the music revolves around the tonic scale degree. The tonic scale degree, which gives us the key of a piece of music, is the most stable of all the degrees, meaning that it brings about a sense of rest. Another way to think of the tonic is to think of it as the music's home. All music consists of going away from and then returning back to that home, its tonic resolution.

The **supertonic** is the second scale degree and is a whole step above the tonic; *super* is Latin for "above."

The **mediant** is the third scale degree and is the very middle note between the tonic and the dominant scale degrees.

Figure 7.3 Major scale degrees

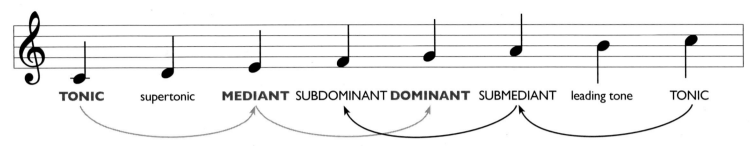

BONUS

Thinking about the scale degrees and their relationships to each other can serve as a memory tool.

The **subdominant** is the fourth scale degree and is right below the dominant scale degree. The prefix *sub–* is Latin for "under" or "lower."

The **dominant** is the fifth scale degree and is called "dominant" because it is the second-most important scale degree behind the tonic scale degree.

The **submediant** is the sixth scale degree and takes its name from the fact that it is the "lower" mediant of the scale, falling in the very middle between the subdominant and the higher tonic scale degrees.

The **leading tone** is the seventh scale degree and is only one half step away from the octave tonic. The leading tone is "leading" into the tonic.

Scale degree numbers and scale degree names stay the same in natural minor scales with only one exception. In a natural minor scale, the seventh scale degree is called the **subtonic**; it is a whole step down from the octave tonic.

Figure 7.4 Natural minor scale degrees

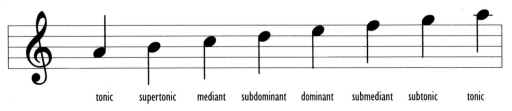

Activity 7.1—In-class activity

Use the blank staff to complete the following:

a) Write a treble clef on the blank staff and include the key signature of D major with a time signature of $\frac{4}{4}$.

b) Write the D major ascending scale on the staff with quarter notes (be sure to use measures appropriately). Begin with the D above middle C.

c) Above each note, write the correct scale degree number, including the caret above each number.

If you are having trouble with the key signatures and scales in this section, go back and review chapters 5 and 6.

BONUS

When notating music, try to point your stems in the direction (up or down) that keeps them within the staff.

Activity 7.2—In-class activity

Use the blank staff to complete the following:

a) Write a treble clef on the blank staff and include the key signature of G minor with a time signature of $\frac{4}{2}$.

b) Write the G natural minor ascending scale on the staff using half notes (be sure to use measures appropriately).

c) Above each note, write the correct scale degree name. Remember, the key is minor.

If you are having trouble with the key signatures and scales in this section, go back and review chapters 5 and 6.

Scale Degrees and Number Transposition

Now that you understand scale degree numbers and names, you can study how to transpose melodies. **Transposition** is the process of rewriting notes at a higher or lower pitch. This process also involves a change in the key signature and pitch, but not the time signature or rhythm. In this chapter, we will learn to do transposition using scale degree numbers and names. Transposition can refer to a scale, a melody, or an entire musical piece, but for now you will learn number transposition through short melodies. A **melody** is a series of single notes used to express a musical idea.

When transposing melodies, there are five basic steps:

1) Know the key of the given melody.

2) Write the scale degree numbers of each note of the given melody.

3) Know the key into which you are transposing and write the key signature.

4) Transfer the scale degree numbers to the new melody.

5) Write the notes of the new melody. It's generally best to write notes that are in the same octave as the original piece.

Now, we'll use these five steps to transpose the melody in Figure 7.5 below into the key of D major.

Figure 7.5

1) The key of the melody below is in C major (no sharps or flats).

2) Write the scale degree numbers under each note of the melody. It may be helpful to write out the C scale and label the scale degrees before beginning.

C	D	E	F	G	A	B	C
$\hat{1}$	$\hat{2}$	$\hat{3}$	$\hat{4}$	$\hat{5}$	$\hat{6}$	$\hat{7}$	$\hat{1}$

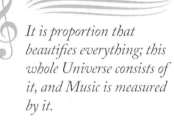

It is proportion that beautifies everything; this whole Universe consists of it, and Music is measured by it.

—Orlando Gibbons

3) The key we are transposing to is D major (two sharps—F♯ and C♯). Write the key signature on the staff for the new melody.

4) Copy the same scale degree numbers onto the staff where the new melody will be written.

Figure 7.6

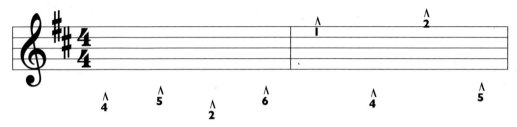

5) Write the notes of the new melody. Again, it may be helpful to write out the scale and scale degree numbers first as a guide for filling in the correct notes of the new, transposed melody.

D	E	F♯	G	A	B	C♯	D
1	2	3	4	5	6	7	1

Figure 7.7

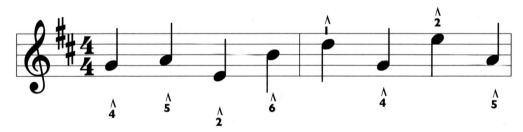

Now that you have learned how to transpose a melody using the five basic steps, put the process into practice with the in-class activity below.

Activity 7.3—In-class activity

Transpose the given melody from the key of A♭ major to the key of B♭ major on the blank staff below. Remember to use the five steps discussed earlier.

Only transpose pitch.
Keep rhythm the same.

Transposition Continued

Another way to think about transposing, or to check the transposition you just did, is to rewrite the melody up or down. For example, if the distance between the original melody and the transposition is a whole step, we can move all notes either up or down accordingly.

Start by knowing the key signature. Next, write the key signature of the new melody. Determine the steps from the original melody to the transposition. Are we moving up one whole step? Down one whole step? Finally, transpose every note of the melody either up or down that same distance.

Look back at the example we did in Figures 7.5, 7.6, and 7.7. We were transposing from C to D, a whole step up. Notice that every note in our new melody is one whole step above the note in the original melody in C major. The first note was an F, now it's a G. The second note was a G, now it's an A, and so on. Figure 7.8 on the next page illustrates this process.

Remember to choose notes that are in the same octave as the original piece.

Figure 7.8

This is very much like algebra, where we can manipulate an equation any way we want, as long as we do the same thing to both sides. In transposition, we can move the melody up or down however we'd like as long as we do it to every note.

In the next chapter on intervals, you will learn how to count the steps between notes greater than a whole step apart, which will enable us to transpose from one key into any other key.

Chapter 7 Review

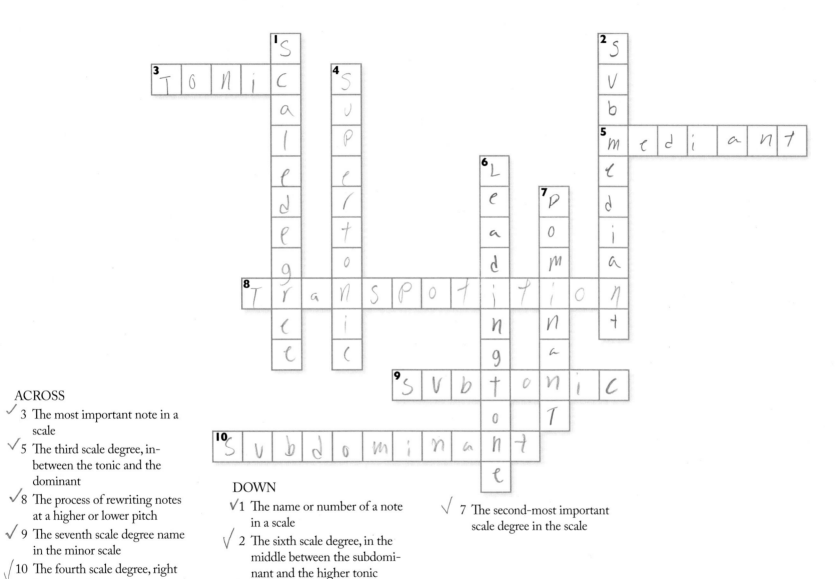

ACROSS

✓ 3 The most important note in a scale

✓ 5 The third scale degree, in-between the tonic and the dominant

✓ 8 The process of rewriting notes at a higher or lower pitch

✓ 9 The seventh scale degree name in the minor scale

✓ 10 The fourth scale degree, right below the dominant

DOWN

✓ 1 The name or number of a note in a scale

✓ 2 The sixth scale degree, in the middle between the subdominant and the higher tonic

✓ 4 The second scale degree, a whole step above the tonic

✓ 6 The seventh scale degree name in the major scale

✓ 7 The second-most important scale degree in the scale

Daily Exercises for Chapter 7

✿ EXERCISES FOR DAY 1

Exercise 7.1

Identify the major key and scale degree numbers for the following excerpts.

1) Bass of "Jesu, Joy of Man's Desiring"

Key: _G Major_

2) First line of "When I Survey the Wondrous Cross"

Key: _F Major_

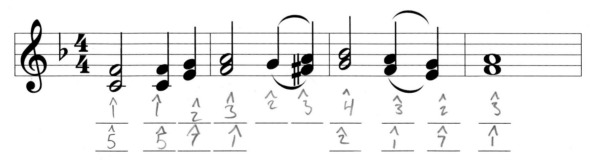

3) First line of "Be Thou My Vision"

Key: _____

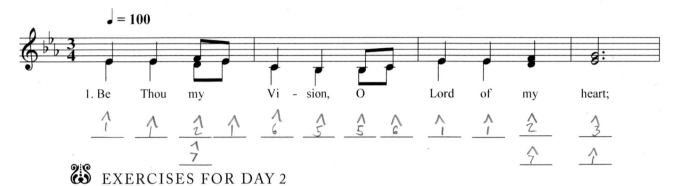

EXERCISES FOR DAY 2

Exercise 7.2

Identify the major key and then write the correct note on the staff from the given scale degree name.

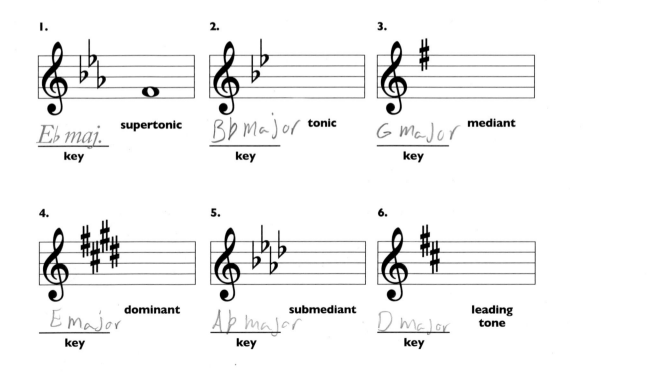

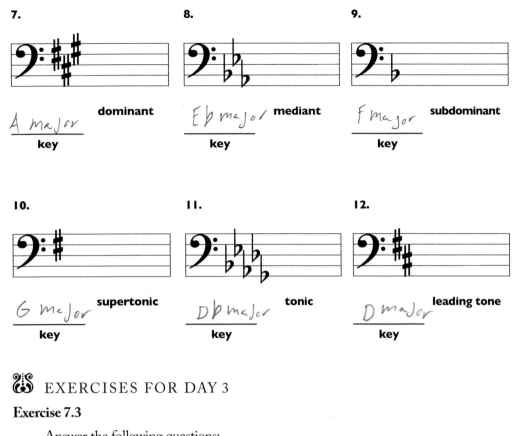

7.

A major — key — dominant

8.

Eb major — key — mediant

9.

F major — key — subdominant

10.

G major — key — supertonic

11.

Db major — key — tonic

12.

D major — key — leading tone

EXERCISES FOR DAY 3

Exercise 7.3

Answer the following questions:

a) Which note is the mediant scale degree in the key of C major?   _E_

b) Which note is the mediant scale degree in the key of C minor?   _Eb_

c) Which note is the leading tone scale degree in the key of D major?   _C#_

d) Which note is the subdominant scale degree in the key of D minor?   _G_

e) Which note is the submediant scale degree in the key of B major?   _G#_

Exercise 7.4

Transpose the melodies below into the requested key.

I. major key of _F major_

key of G major

2. major key of _D major_

key of C major

Using the blank staff below, compose a melody that fits the time signature.

3. key of B♭

Now transpose your melody above to the key of A major.

❧ EXERCISES FOR DAY 4

Exercise 7.5

Identify the correct scale degree name for the circled notes in the excerpt from "Be Thou My Vision."

major key: ___Eb Major___

1) ___dominant___   6) ___mediant___

2) ___dominant___   7) ___Sub dominant___

3) ___Sub dominant___   8) ___tonic___

4) ___Mediant___   9) ___Super tonic___

5) ___tonic___   10) ___dominant___

Exercise 7.6

Transpose the first line of the hymn "There Is a Fountain" into the key of C major. Remember that transposition only changes the pitch; it does not adjust the time signature or rhythm.

There Is a Fountain

ZECHARIAH 13:1
William Cowper, *pub.*1772

CLEANSING FOUNTAIN
attr. to Lowell Mason

1. There   is   a foun - tain filled with blood, Drawn from Im - man - uel's veins,
2. The   dy - ing thief re - joiced to see That foun - tain in His day;
3. Dear   dy - ing Lamb, Thy pre - cious blood Shall nev - er lose its pow'r,
4. E'er   since by faith I saw the stream Thy flow - ing wounds sup - ply,
5. When   this poor, lisp - ing, stam - m'ring tongue Lies si - lent in the grave,

Intervals

In the last chapter, you learned about scale degrees and number transposition. In this chapter, you will learn types of intervals in a context of major scales and keys. These intervals are critical for understanding the concepts discussed in chapters 9 and 10.

Harmonic & Melodic Intervals

An **interval** is the distance between two notes or two pitches.

Figure 8.1

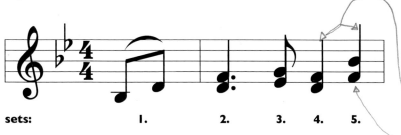

sets: 1.   2.   3.   4.   5.

Figure 8.1 shows the beginning measures from the score "There Is a Fountain."

When two notes are played at the same time, it is called a **harmonic interval**. In set 2, the D and F are a harmonic interval because they are played at the same time.

When one note occurs after another note, it is called a **melodic interval**. In set 1, the B♭ and D make a melodic interval.

Melodic intervals may be either ascending or descending.

The rotation of the universe and the motion of the planets could neither begin nor continue without music… for everything is ordered …according to the laws of harmony.

—Quote attributed to Plutarch

⚡ Interval Size ⚡

There are two parts to identifying intervals: *size* and *quality*. **Interval size** is the number of lines and spaces, or letter names, represented on the staff. When counting size you always include the first and last notes. For example, the interval in Figure 8.2 is called a second (2nd) since G is one line/space and letter name and A is another line/space and letter name. Think of interval size in the same way you would think of ordinal numbers: first, second, third, etc.

Figure 8.2

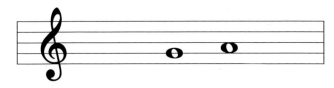

There are eight different size options from a given starting note to its octave. Figure 8.3 illustrates this from the starting note F. These eight intervals are referred to as **simple intervals** because they are within an octave of the starting pitch.

BONUS

An interval in which successive notes lie on the same line or space in a given staff is called a **unison interval**.

Figure 8.3

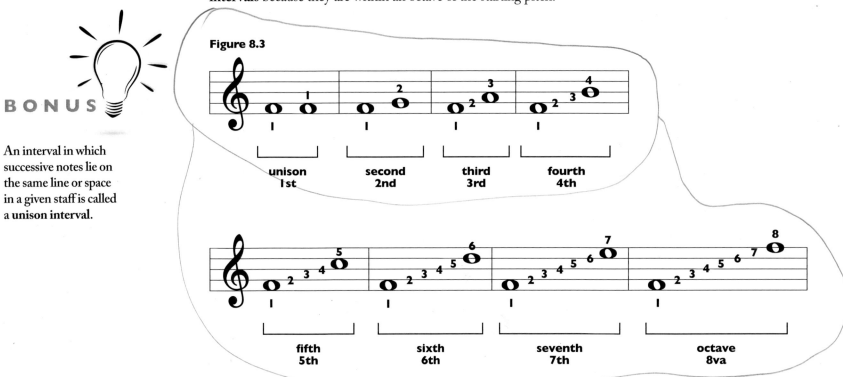

As you will notice, the number of lines and spaces, or letter names, starting on the beginning note and ending on the final note, determines the name of the interval size. In measure five, for example, the number of lines and spaces including the beginning and ending notes, is 5 (F, G, A, B, C); thus, the interval size is a fifth (5th or 5).

The size of an interval is not dependent on the type of interval, harmonic or melodic, or whether the melodic interval is ascending or descending. An interval is always measured from the lower note to the upper note. The size of each interval in Figure 8.4 is a fourth, four lines and spaces. See how the size, the number of lines and spaces, remains the same regardless of whether or not the interval is harmonic or melodic, ascending or descending?

Figure 8.4

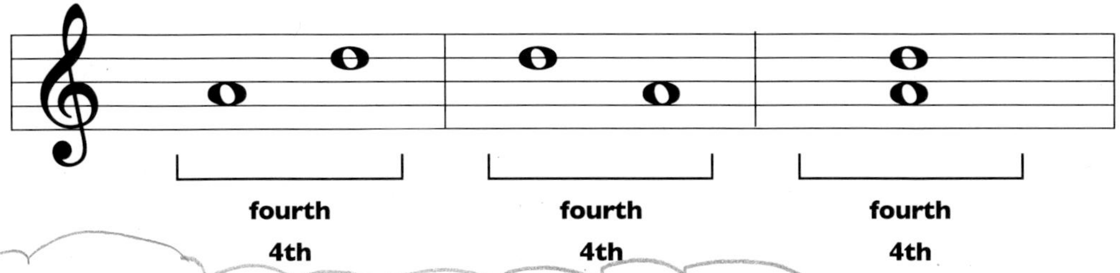

Activity 8.1—In-class activity

Identify the size of the intervals below.

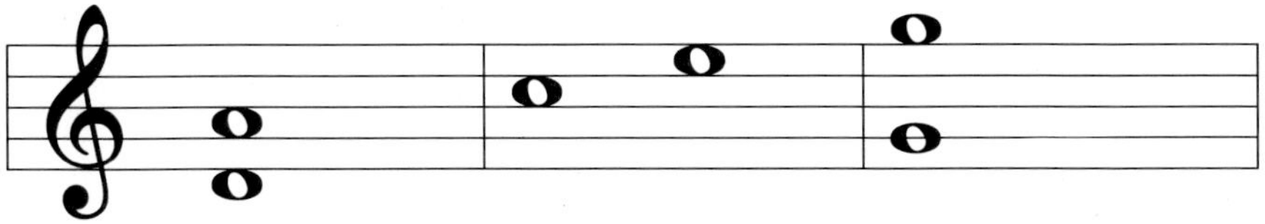

5th 3rd 8va

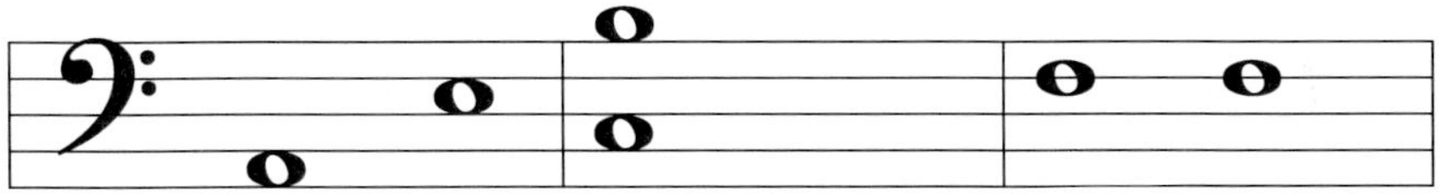

6th 7th 1 unison

Interval Quality

Understanding interval size is an important step for reading and writing intervals. But understanding interval size alone is not enough. For example, the two figures below show intervals of a third, three lines and spaces, but they would not sound the same if they were played. Why do you think that is?

Figure 8.5

Figure 8.6

The flat means that the notes played together in Figure 8.6 would sound different from the notes played together in Figure 8.5. This means that size alone is not enough to fully explain intervals. We need to explore the other part of intervals: *interval quality*.

The **interval quality** denotes the specific type of relationship between two notes. Unlike the size of an interval, which only denotes the number of lines and spaces, the quality, when coupled with size, deals with the exact distance between two notes. Interval quality can be *minor, major, perfect, diminished,* or *augmented* depending on the interval size.

Natural Intervals

In chapters 5 and 6, you learned the major and natural minor scales, and the key signatures associated with those scale types. Major scales and key signatures are extremely important when learning interval qualities. The more you know your major scales, and the key signature coupled with them, the more successful you will be at recognizing intervals.

Each ascending note in a given major scale is either major or perfect as it relates to the tonic. These interval relationships are called **natural intervals** because they are a "natural" part of the major scales. Furthermore, these natural interval qualities, major and perfect, can only occur on specific interval sizes. The chart below illustrates this concept.

Interval Sizes		Natural Interval Quality
2nd, 3rd, 6th, 7th	Are	Major
Unison, 4th, 5th, 8*va*	Are	Perfect

In order to see natural intervals and their relationships, let's use the note C and the C major scale and key. The C major scale consists of the following notes in order: C, D, E, F, G, A, B, and C. In Figure 8.7, the distance starting on C and going up to F is called a is a fourth.

The trouble with music appreciation in general is that people are taught to have too much respect for music; they should be taught to love it instead.

—Igor Stravinsky (1964)

Since all natural intervals are either major or perfect, and this interval is a fourth in size, the chart indicates that it must be perfect. In the same figure, the distance starting on C and going up to E is called a major third. It spans three lines and spaces and is a natural interval, therefore the chart indicates that it is major.

Figure 8.7

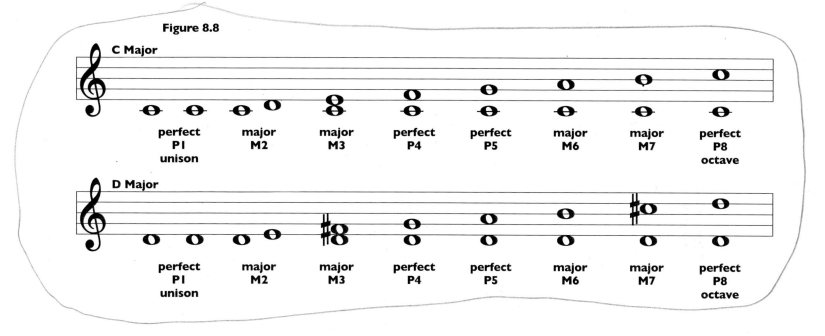

All major keys have the same pattern of major and perfect intervals.

Compare the interval qualities in each of the major scales in Figure 8.8. Notice that the pattern is the same in each one.

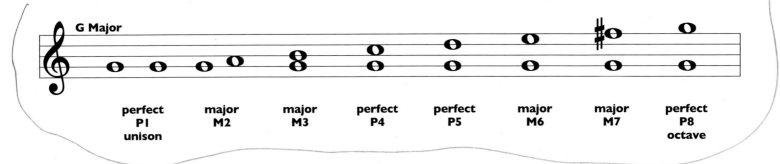

To identify interval quality, you will need to be extremely familiar with major scales and key signatures, as you will always use the key of the lower note to help you with the identification. To see this more fully, let's try to identify the interval in Figure 8.9. To begin, we should start with the size. Starting with the lowest note F, we count up to the higher note D; in so doing, we find that there are six lines and spaces between the two notes and thus the size of sixth is given. To identify the quality, we must consider the major key and scale of the lower note. The key of F major contains the following notes: F–G–A–B♭–C–D–E–F. The upper note, D, is part of the F major scale, so the interval of F–D is a natural interval. As a sixth, it is major in quality. Therefore, the interval is a major sixth.

Figure 8.9

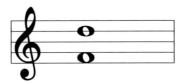

major sixth (often abbreviated as M6)

Let's try to identify another interval in Figure 8.10. Again, always begin with size when identifying an interval. Starting on the lower note A♭ and counting up to the top note D♭, you find that there are four lines and spaces between theses note. The size is therefore a fourth. When looking at the quality, you use the major key and scale of the lower note. The A♭ major scale contains the notes A♭–B♭–C–D♭–E♭–F–G–A♭. We know that when the upper note is part of the major scale of the lower note, the interval is a natural interval and will be major or perfect. A fourth is perfect, so this interval is a perfect fourth.

Figure 8.10

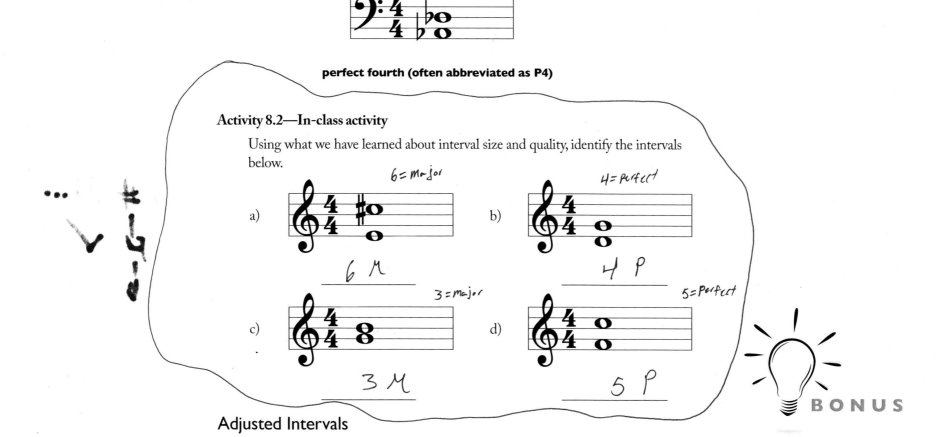

perfect fourth (often abbreviated as P4)

Activity 8.2—In-class activity

Using what we have learned about interval size and quality, identify the intervals below.

a) 6 M

b) 4 P

c) 3 M

d) 5 P

Adjusted Intervals

At this point, we have come to understand intervals by size and quality. Thus far, the quality has been determined by whether the top note is part of the major key or scale of the lower note. When this is the case, the interval quality is either major or perfect. However, what do we do if the top note is outside the major key or scale of the lower note? This leads us to adjusted intervals. **Adjusted intervals** occur when the higher note is outside the major key or scale of the lower note. These adjustments outside the key give us three additional interval qualities: **minor, augmented**, and **diminished**. The adjustment outside the key is expressed in terms of half steps from the natural interval position. The name of the adjustment is different depending on what type (major or perfect) of natural interval is being changed. Figure 8.11 illustrates how half-step adjustments to the top note change the quality.

BONUS

"Augment" is from the Latin root *augere*, meaning "to raise or increase."

"Diminish" is from the Latin root *diminuere*, meaning "to lessen or diminish."

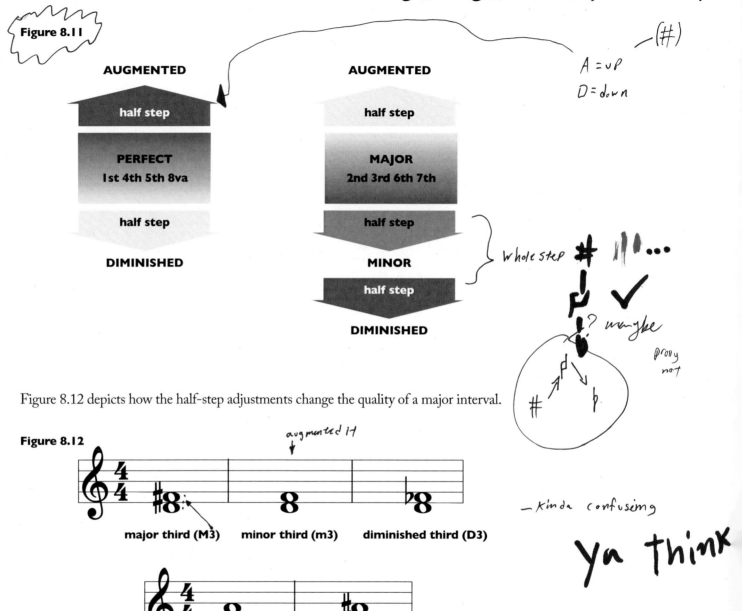

Figure 8.11

— (#)

A = up
D = down

AUGMENTED

half step

PERFECT
1st 4th 5th 8va

half step

DIMINISHED

AUGMENTED

half step

MAJOR
2nd 3rd 6th 7th

half step

MINOR

half step

DIMINISHED

whole step # ¶ ...

? maybe

prolly not

Figure 8.12 depicts how the half-step adjustments change the quality of a major interval.

Figure 8.12

augmented 14

major third (M3) minor third (m3) diminished third (D3)

major third (M3) augmented third (A3)

— kinda confusing

ya think

In measure one of Figure 8.12, the interval is a major third (M3). You know this because the size between D and F♯ is a third and because F♯ is part of the D major scale and key. If we lower the top note by one half step from F♯, it becomes an F♮. This adjustment changes the quality from major to minor. In fact, whenever we lower the top note of a major interval by a half step, it becomes a **minor interval**. Thus, the interval in measure two is called a minor third (m3).

If we lower the F by one half step, as shown in the third measure, it becomes an F♭. This adjustment changes the quality from minor to diminished. The interval in measure three is therefore a diminished third (D3). In fact, whenever we lower the top note of a perfect or minor interval by one half step, it becomes a **diminished interval**.

Measure four shows a major third, F to A. If we raise the top note of a major or perfect interval by one half step, it becomes an **augmented interval**. These adjustments will be true for all major intervals regardless of size.

Figure 8.13

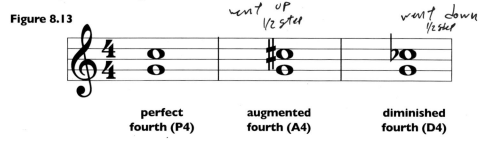

perfect
fourth (P4)   augmented
                     fourth (A4)   diminished
                                          fourth (D4)

For an illustration of these relationships, refer back to Figure 8.11.

When perfect intervals are adjusted, the qualities follow a different pattern. As Figure 8.13 shows, the G to C in measure one is a perfect fourth (P4). We can quickly identify this interval as a fourth because there are four lines and spaces when starting on G and moving up to C. We also know that the quality is perfect because C is in the key/scale of G major. When we raise the top note by one half step from C to C♯, the interval becomes augmented in quality. The interval in measure two is therefore an augmented fourth (A4). When we lower the top note by one half step from C to C♭, it becomes diminished in quality. The interval in measure three is a diminished fourth (D4).

Activity 8.3—In-class activity

Using what we have learned about interval size and quality, identify the intervals below. Remember to use the key of the lower note even if that differs from the given key signature.

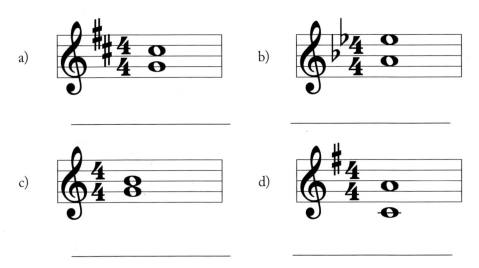

a)

b)

c)

d)

Compound and Simple Intervals

As mentioned earlier, intervals with a size of eight or less are called **simple intervals**. Intervals with a size greater than an octave are called **compound intervals**.

Figure 8.14

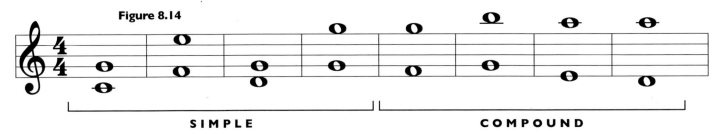

SIMPLE   COMPOUND

Compound intervals have size and quality, just as simple intervals do. To determine the size of a compound interval, count the number of lines and spaces just as you do with simple intervals, starting on the beginning note and ending on the final note. In Figure 8.14 above, the first compound interval is a ninth (F G A B C D E F G). The second compound interval is a tenth (G A B C D E F G A B), and so on.

To find the quality of a compound interval, think of it as a simple interval. The quality of the simple interval is the same as the quality of the compound interval. In other words, reduce the interval to a simple interval and find the quality as in the example below.

Figure 8.15

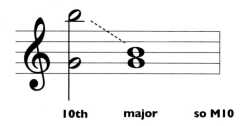

10th   major   so M10

Chapter 8 Review

_e_ 1. Interval

_h_ 2. Harmonic interval

_c_ 3. Melodic interval

_f_ 4. Interval size

_b_ 5. Interval quality

_g_ 6. Augmented

_n_ 7. Diminished

_m_ 8. Simple interval

_k_ 9. Compound interval

_a_ 10. Major sixth

_j_ 11. Minor sixth

_p_ 12. Perfect fourth

_o_ 13. Perfect fifth

_l_ 14. Diminished fifth

_d_ 15. Natural interval

_i_ 16. Adjusted interval

a. C–A interval quality

b. Denotes the specific type of relationship between two notes

c. When one note occurs after another note

d. An interval that is a natural part of a major scale

e. The distance between two notes or two pitches

f. The number of lines and spaces, or letter names, represented on the staff

g. A major or perfect interval that has been raised by a half step

h. When two notes are played at the same time

i. An interval that occurs when the higher note is outside of the key or scale of the lower note

j. E–C quality interval

k. An interval with a size greater than an octave

l. C–G♭ quality interval

m. An interval within an octave of the starting pitch

n. A perfect or minor interval that has been lowered by a half step

o. F–C interval quality

p. C–F interval quality

Daily Exercises for Chapter 8

𝄢 EXERCISES FOR DAY 1

Exercise 8.1

Read through chapter 8 and answer the following questions:

a) What is an interval?

distance between 2 notes or 2 pitches

b) What is the difference between (interval size) and (interval quality?) *— specific type of relationship between 2 notes*

# of lines + spaces + letter names represented on staff

c) What is the difference between harmonic and melodic intervals?

2 notes at the same time   *one note after the other*

d) What is the difference between simple and compound intervals?

within an octave of starting pitch   *interval w/ a size of more than an octave*

e) What prior knowledge of music theory is important for determining interval qualities?

Knowledge of major scales and key signature is important for that

Exercise 8.2

Use the measures below to answer the questions that follow.

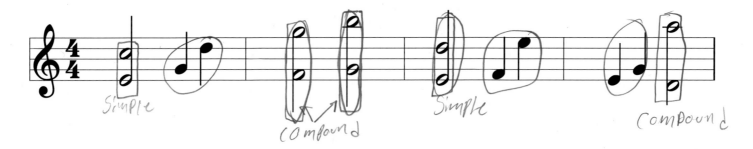

a) Circle the melodic intervals in the measures above.

b) Place a box around the harmonic intervals in the measures above.

c) Label the harmonic intervals that are also simple intervals.

d) Label the harmonic intervals that are also compound intervals.

EXERCISES FOR DAY 2

Exercise 8.3

Identify the size of the intervals below.

4th   7th   5th   5th   6th   2nd   8va   3rd

5th   3rd   6th   2nd   8va   7th   4th   5th

Exercise 8.4

Identify the following intervals including size and quality. Remember to use the key of the lowest note even if it differs from the given key signature.

M3   P5   M7   M9   P4   M6   P8   P4

EXERCISES FOR DAY 3

Exercise 8.5

Identify the following intervals as minor or major third intervals (M3 or m3).
Remember to use the key signature of the lower note.

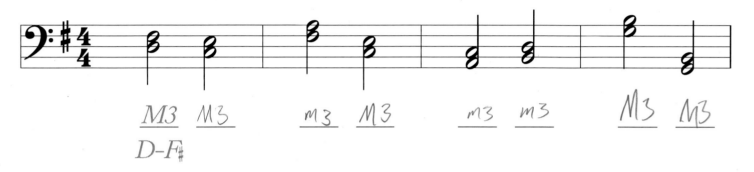

M3   M3   m3   M3   m3   m3   M3   M3

D-F♯

Identify the following intervals as minor or major sixth intervals (m6 or M6). Remember to use the key signature of the lower note.

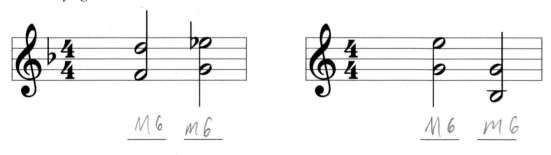

M6   m6   M6   M6

Exercise 8.6

Identify the following intervals as minor or major seventh intervals. Remember to use the key signature of the lower note.

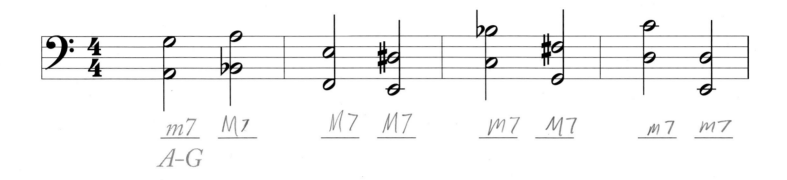

m7   M7   M7   M7   m7   M7   m7   m7

A–G

Identify the following intervals as perfect, augmented, or diminished fifths (P5) or fourths (P4). Remember to use the key signature of the lower note.

A5   P5   P4   d5

EXERCISES FOR DAY 4

Exercise 8.7

Identify the following intervals below by quality. Remember, even though a key signature is given, you must always use the key of the lower note.

Excerpt of the first line from "When I Survey the Wondrous Cross"

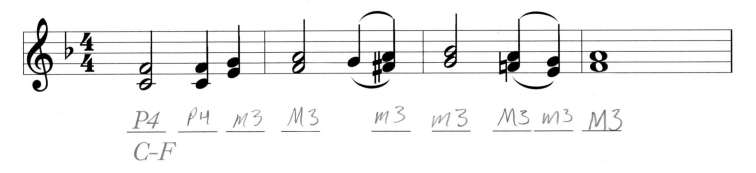

P4   P4   m3   M3   m3   m3   M3 m3   M3

C–F

Excerpt of the treble clef from the last line of "There Is a Fountain"

m6 M6   M6   m6 M6 M6   P5   m3   M3

D–B♭   *melodic*

Exercise 8.8

Identify the following melodic intervals below by quality. Remember, even though a key signature is given, you must always use the key of the lower note.

Excerpt of the bass clef from the first line of "Jesu, Joy of Man's Desiring"

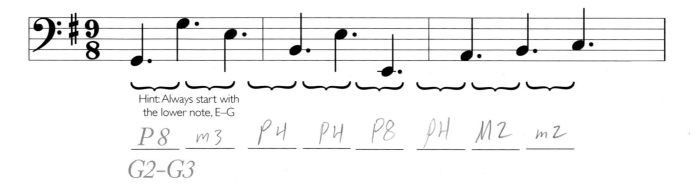

Hint: Always start with the lower note, E–G

P8   m3   P4   P4   P8   P4   M2   m2

G2–G3

9 Triads and Triad Qualities

Since you have a good grasp on interval qualities, you are now ready to apply your understanding to triads and triad qualities. Triads (and other chords) are part of the necessary context for applying your study of intervals.

In this chapter, you will learn about chords, triads, and the triad qualities of *major*, *minor*, *diminished*, and *augmented*. Understanding the fundamentals of triads is crucial in score analysis. This chapter will give you the tools to appreciate many styles of Western music and the concepts behind them.

Chords and Triads

Most modern Western music is written in a series of chords. **Chords** are a harmonious group of notes that can be played together or separately. When the notes of a chord are broken up and played one after another in sequence, they are called an **arpeggio**.

In Western music, chords are built upwards from a root. In this chapter you will learn about the simplest kind of chord, the **triad**, so named because it is formed with three notes: the **root** (foundational note), a third (three lines and spaces above the root), and a fifth (five lines and spaces above the root). This is the most fundamental harmonic group in tonal music.

Figure 9.1

When the root, third, and fifth are written on the staff, the triad occurs on three successive lines or three successive spaces.

Triad Qualities

There are four qualities of the triad, which correspond to the qualities of intervals in the last chapter: *major, minor, diminished,* and *augmented.*

These four qualities depend on the qualities of the thirds and fifths within the triad.

Major triads are built with the *major* third and the *perfect* fifth.

Minor triads are built with the *minor* third and the *perfect* fifth.

Diminished triads are built with the *minor* third and the *diminished* fifth.

Augmented triads are built with the *major* third and the *augmented* fifth.

As an example, notice these four qualities of triads from the root C in Figure 9.2:

Figure 9.2

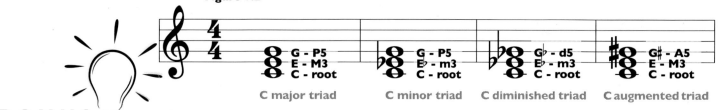

C major triad   C minor triad   C diminished triad   C augmented triad

generic *(adj.)* Characteristic relating to a group of things; not specific

Since triad quality is determined by the specific combination of thirds and fifths above the root, any note can be chosen as a root and, using the correct combination of third and fifth, any quality can be created. For example, suppose that you would like to create a diminished triad that has A as its root. Begin by adding two notes—a generic third and fifth above the root—to the existing note and thus create the triad.

Figure 9.3

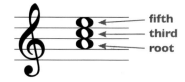

fifth
third
root

BONUS

Next, add sharps or flats to the third and fifth so that the notes within the triad conform to the pattern presented for a diminished chord: a minor third and diminished fifth above the root. Using the techniques discussed in chapter 8, you are able discern that the distance from A to C is a minor third and A to E is a perfect fifth. Therefore, you must add the E♭ to the existing triad to ensure that the quality matches the pattern for a diminished triad.

Figure 9.4

Qui bene cantat, bis orat *(He who sings well prays twice.)*

—Quote often attributed to St. Augustine of Hippo

To apply this process to a different starting note or to create a different triad quality, simply insert a generic third and fifth above the root and apply the appropriate sharps or flats as the patterns for the specific quality prescribes.

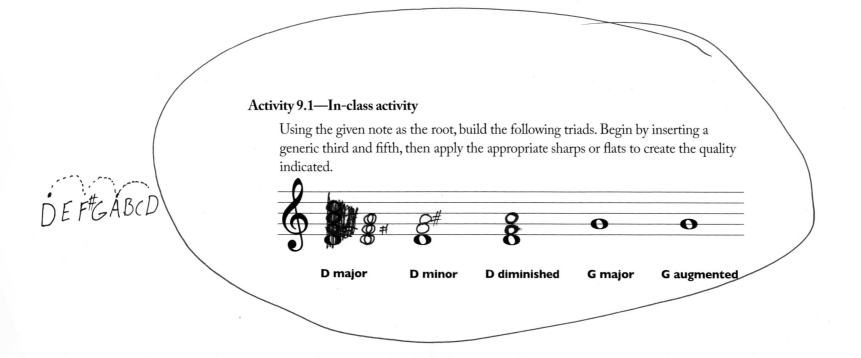

Activity 9.1—In-class activity

Using the given note as the root, build the following triads. Begin by inserting a generic third and fifth, then apply the appropriate sharps or flats to create the quality indicated.

Roots and Chord Symbols

The root note of the triad is important because it determines how the triad is named. For example, a B major triad has the note B as its root, the D♯ as its third, and the F♯ as its fifth. Look at the B major triad on the keyboard in Figure 9.5.

Figure 9.5

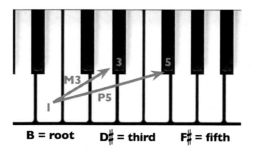

B = root   D♯ = third   F♯ = fifth

Figure 9.5 gives us the relationships between the three notes of the B major triad. The B root and the D♯ third is a major third interval. The B root and the F♯ fifth is a perfect fifth interval.

This triad is major because the distance between the root and the third note is a major third and the distance between the root and the fifth is a perfect fifth, thus conforming with the pattern for a major triad. If we were to change the D♯ to a D natural, this triad would be a B minor triad (B–D–F♯).

The importance of triad roots becomes apparent when attempting to name the chord. As mentioned above, the letter name of the root is used to describe the chord (see Figure 9.5); however, the letter name alone is not sufficient, as it does not discuss quality. Thus composers and performers of all styles of music will often use chord symbols to denote in shorthand a particular triad.

Major chords will often use a capital letter of the root to signify "major." **F** (F Major)

Minor chords will use a capital letter of the root including a lowercase "m" to signify "minor." **Fm** (F minor)

Diminished chords will use a capital letter of the root followed by a small circle to signify "diminished." **F∘** (F diminished)

Augmented chords will use a capital letter of the root followed by a plus sign to signify "augmented." **F+** (F augmented)

Figure 9.6 Chord symbols for triads

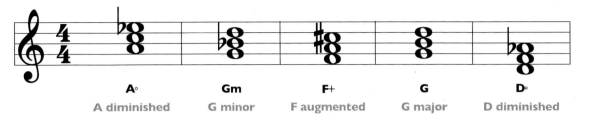

Diatonic Triads

Diatonic triads are triads that use only the notes, including sharps or flats, of a given scale. For example, if we formed triads on every note in the key of D, we would form triads on the following notes: D–E–F♯–G–A–B–C♯–D. In doing so, we discover the chord qualities for each of the notes in a scale.

Figure 9.7 Diatonic triads in the key of D

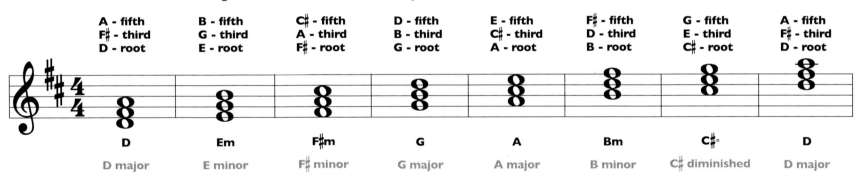

Notice that there are no accidentals used in any of the chords, because these are all the diatonic triads of the key of D major. In other words, we only apply the sharps found within the key signature to our triads. We have not added any accidentals to our triads that are not already found in the key of D major. We thus use those, and only those, sharps or flats already in the key signature to help us discern chord quality. For example, the triad built on the tonic, D, is D-F♯-A.

In addition, the triad qualities within a given major or minor key are the same for all major and minor keys. In other words, when triads are built from the notes of a scale or key, the triad qualities will always follow the same pattern, regardless of the scale. For example, in Figure 9.7 the second triad, E, is minor in quality. In Figure 9.8 the second triad in the key of G major, A, is minor in quality. Compare the triads built on each scale degree of the D major and G major scales. You should find that the qualities are the same for both (third scale degree is minor, fourth is major, etc.). This is true in all major and minor keys (although we will discuss minor later).

Figure 9.8 Diatonic triads in the key of G major

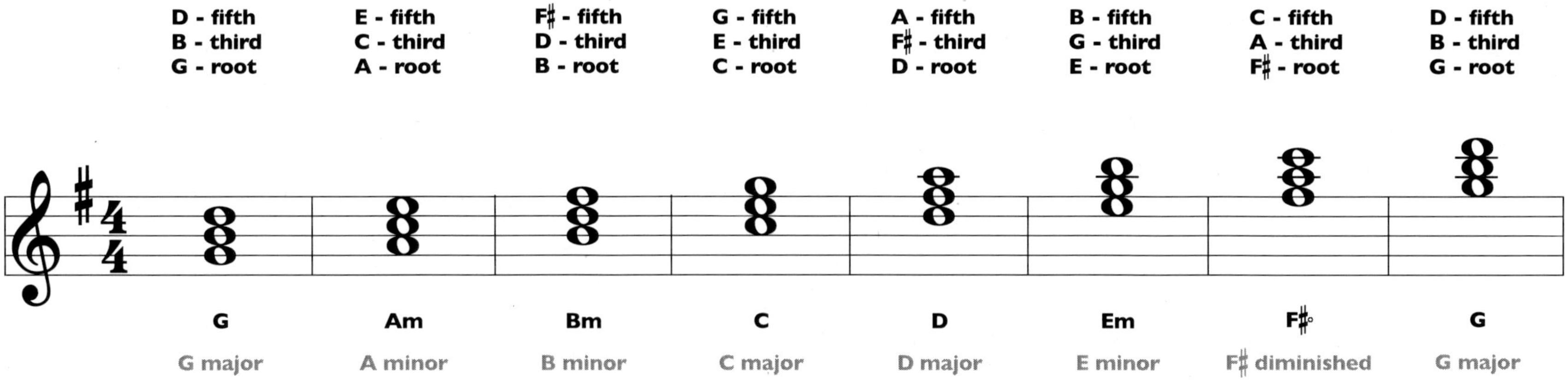

Arpeggiated Triads

Of course, triads do not always appear in neat stacks on the staff. Often, they are arranged in different melodic structures such as arpeggios. Arpeggios are the notes of a chord broken from their stack and played in sequence. For instance, see the next page for examples of arpeggiated triads in Figure 9.9.

Figure 9.9

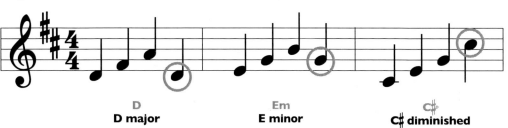

In Figure 9.9, each triad has been arpeggiated so that the notes are not played simultaneously, but they are still triads. When a note is repeated in an arpeggio above, it has been
circled. The name or quality of a triad does not change if one of its notes is doubled, since a
triad is a harmonious grouping and not a specific order of notes. A famous classical piece in
which arpeggiation is used is Beethoven's Piano Sonata No. 14, Op. 27 No.2, often referred
to as the "Moonlight Sonata." Try to find a recording of this song and listen to it so you can
understand how arpeggios sound. The song "Jesu, Joy of Man's Desiring" is also an example
of the use of arpeggios. This piece is included in the anthology of hymn scores in the back
of this book. Try to find a recording of it and read the music while you listen to it.

A Quality

Which music sometimes has,
being the Art

Which is most nigh to tears
and memory.

—Oscar Wilde

Activity 9.2—In-class activity

Use the given note as the root to arpeggiate the major triads in Figure 9.10a and the minor triads in Figure 9.10b. Finish each measure by adding extra notes or changing note values to fit the meter. If you add an extra note, be sure that the note is in the same major or minor triad.

Figure 9.10a

Example: D major triad

Figure 9.10b

Example: E minor triad

Chapter 9 Review

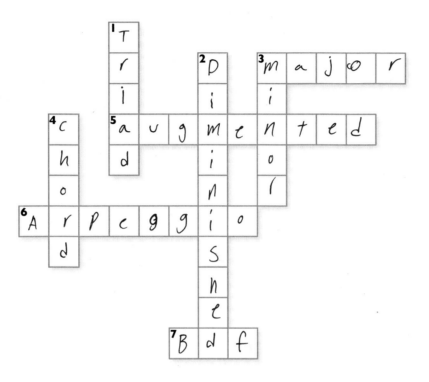

ACROSS

3 Triad built with a major third and perfect fifth

5 Triad built with a major third and an augmented fifth

6 The notes of a chord are broken up and played in sequence

7 The B diminished triad contains these notes

DOWN

1 Chord formed with three notes consisting of the root, the third from the root, and the fifth from the root

2 Triad built with a minor third and a diminished fifth

3 Triad built with a minor third and a perfect fifth

4 A harmonious group of notes played together or separately

Daily Exercises for Chapter 9

EXERCISES FOR DAY 1

Exercise 9.1

Read through chapter 9 and answer the following questions:

a) What is the difference between a chord and a triad?

a chord is a harmonious group of notes
a triad is a 3 note chord consisting of the root, third, and fifth

b) What is an arpeggio?

when the notes of a chord are broken up and
played one after the other in sequence, they are called arpeggio

c) What are the four qualities of triads?

major, minor, augmented, diminished

d) Give the symbols of the four qualities of triads. Use G as the root in your
examples.

G (major)   Gm (minor)   G⁺ (augmented)   G∘ (diminished)

e) Give the qualities of the intervals included in a major triad.

major third, and perfect fifth

f) Give the qualities of the intervals included in a minor triad.

minor third and perfect fifth

Exercise 9.2

Supply the missing note in each triad to complete each of the triads below. Pay close attention to the quality indicated.

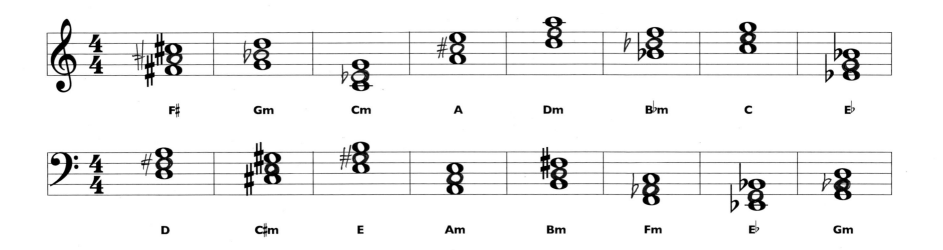

EXERCISES FOR DAY 2

Exercise 9.3

Supply the missing note (fifth) in each triad to complete each of the triads below. Pay close attention to the quality indicated.

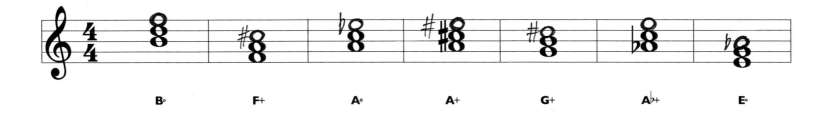

Exercise 9.4

Finish the indicated quality triads below.

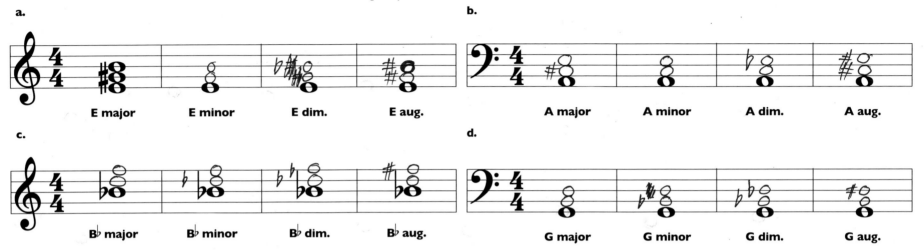

Exercise 9.5

Identify the quality of the triads below as major, minor, diminished, or augmented by using the root and correct chord symbol.

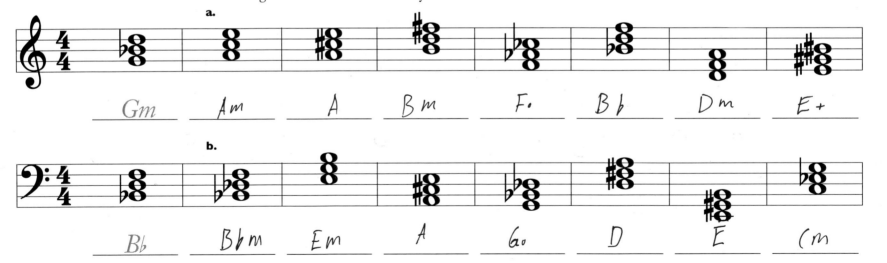

EXERCISES FOR DAY 3

Exercise 9.6

Correctly add sharps or flats to complete the requested qualities of the triads below.

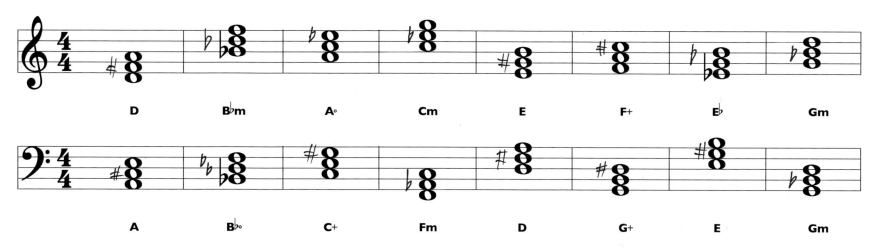

Exercise 9.7

Supply the missing notes to complete each of the triads below. Pay close attention to the quality indicated. The given note is the root.

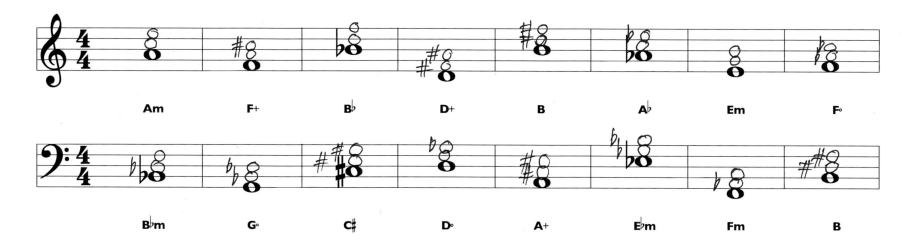

✤ EXERCISES FOR DAY 4

Exercise 9.8

Supply the missing notes to complete each of the triads below. Pay close attention to the quality indicated. The given note is the fifth, not the root. The first one is done for you.

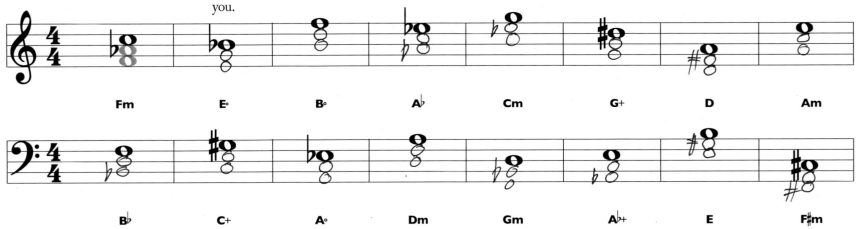

Fm   E°   B°   A♭   Cm   G+   D   Am

B♭   C+   A°   Dm   Gm   A♭+   E   F♯m

Exercise 9.9

Supply the missing notes to complete each of the triads below. For each triad, you are given a note, its position within the triad, and the triad quality. The first one is done for you.

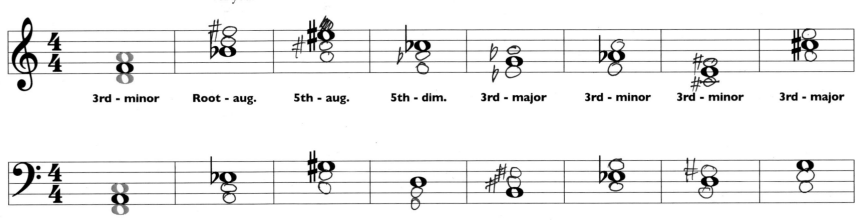

3rd - minor   Root - aug.   5th - aug.   5th - dim.   3rd - major   3rd - minor   3rd - minor   3rd - major

3rd - major   5th - dim.   5th - aug.   5th - major   Root - major   3rd - minor   3rd - minor   5th - major

10 Triads: Roman Numeral Analysis

The theory behind Western music began with the Greek philosopher Pythagoras, who discovered how certain ratios in the physical world relate to musical harmony. For example, a plucked string makes a certain tone. Pythagoras discovered that if he cut that string in half and plucked it again, it would make a tone exactly one octave higher. This harmonic order was developed throughout the Greek and medieval periods and was further expanded in the modern era, from the sixteenth century to the present. Throughout these eras, the basic principle of tonality that Pythagoras discovered provided the foundation on which music developed into a system of greater and greater complexity. **Tonality** is the principle of organization of a work around a tonic, which provides a context for the harmonic movement of the whole piece.

The tonal principle is clearly seen in the organization of triads. The C major triad finds its tonal center in the root C, which provides context for the other notes of the chord. Without the C, you would not know in which key the notes belonged. In the same way, without a clear tonic, harmonic movement in a whole piece of music loses much of its meaning and purpose.

Figure 10.1

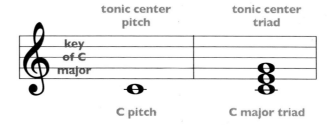

Triad Degrees in Major Keys

As briefly discussed in chapter 9, we can create diatonic triads in any major or minor key. Furthermore, we learned that when doing so we use only the sharps or flats already present in the given key. Since we only use the notes present in the scale, whether major or minor, we also create triads in which the root corresponds with the scale degree names discussed in chapter 7. For example, Figure 10.2 illustrates triads that are all built on the notes of the G major scale. The scale degree names are also used to describe diatonic triads since the relationship to the key and tonic center is the same as the relationships of the scale degrees.

Figure 10.2 Triads named by scale degrees and qualities

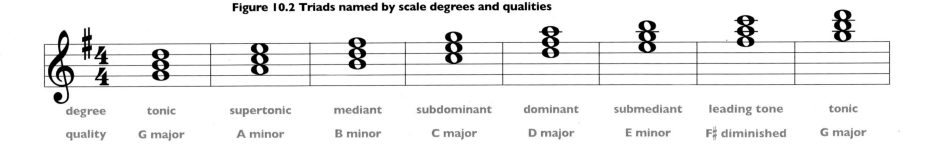

degree	tonic	supertonic	mediant	subdominant	dominant	submediant	leading tone	tonic
quality	G major	A minor	B minor	C major	D major	E minor	F♯ diminished	G major

Again, the scale degree names and qualities in Figure 10.2 apply equally to triads in all major keys; in essence they follow a pattern.

Major Scale Degree Name	**Major Triad Qualities**
tonic	major
supertonic	minor
median	minor
subdominant	major
dominant	major
submediant	minor
leading tone	diminished
tonic	major

This pattern of diatonic triad qualities applies to all major keys regardless of starting note.

Triads in Minor Keys

Minor keys also have a consistent pattern of diatonic triads; however, there are differences in the name of the seventh scale degree and the qualities of the triads. In the major key, the seventh scale degree—and thus the triad on that scale degree—is called the leading tone. In the minor key, the seventh scale degree and accompanying triad is called the subtonic. The qualities of the triads in a minor key differ from those in a major key.

Figure 10.3 E minor triads named by scale degrees and qualities

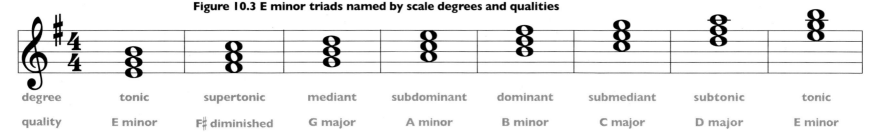

degree	tonic	supertonic	mediant	subdominant	dominant	submediant	subtonic	tonic
quality	E minor	F# diminished	G major	A minor	B minor	C major	D major	E minor

Compare the tonic triad in Figures 10.2 and 10.3. Notice that the quality of the tonic triad in a major key (Figure 10.2) is major, while the quality of the tonic triad in a minor key (Figure 10.3) is minor.

Take a close look at the chart below to see the pattern of scale degree names and qualities for a minor key.

Minor Scale Degree Name	Minor Scale Degree Chord Qualities
tonic	minor
supertonic	diminished
mediant	major
subdominant	minor
dominant	minor
submediant	major
subtonic	major
tonic	minor

The order of these qualities serves as a pattern for all minor keys. Thus, the triads in all minor keys will follow the same order: the first chord will be minor, the second diminished, and so on. This pattern of triad qualities is based on the natural minor scale. If you want to know more about the pattern of triads based on the harmonic and melodic minor scales, refer to the Supplemental Material section.

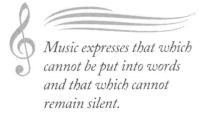

Music expresses that which cannot be put into words and that which cannot remain silent.

—Victor Hugo

Analysis with Roman Numerals

While scale degrees and qualities can be helpful in understanding the triad and its relationship to the tonic, there is another, and perhaps better, way to name triads: Roman numerals. Roman numerals are helpful because they can communicate a number of different ideas about the notes of a piece of music. **Roman numeral analysis** is a form of harmonic analysis where Roman numerals are used to represent different chords in a given score.

Roman numerals communicate

1) the scale degree number,

2) the scale degree name, and

3) the quality of the chord.

Roman numerals can also be easily adjusted to communicate notes or chords outside the key.

diatonic = notes that you'll find in G Major Scale

Figure 10.4 Roman numeral analysis with triads in the key of C major

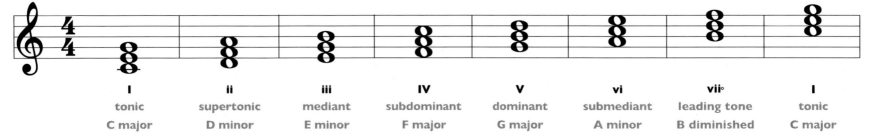

I	ii	iii	IV	V	vi	vii°	I
tonic	supertonic	mediant	subdominant	dominant	submediant	leading tone	tonic
C major	D minor	E minor	F major	G major	A minor	B diminished	C major

You will notice in the example above that there are capital and lowercase Roman numerals. Capital Roman numerals refer to the major triads, and lowercase ones refer to the minor triads. The diminished triads are lowercase letters with a ° sign. When augmented triads are used, the letters are capital and include a + sign.

Remember that triad qualities follow the same pattern, regardless of the scale. Compare the Roman numerals in the G major scale in Figure 10.5 to the C major scale in Figure 10.4.

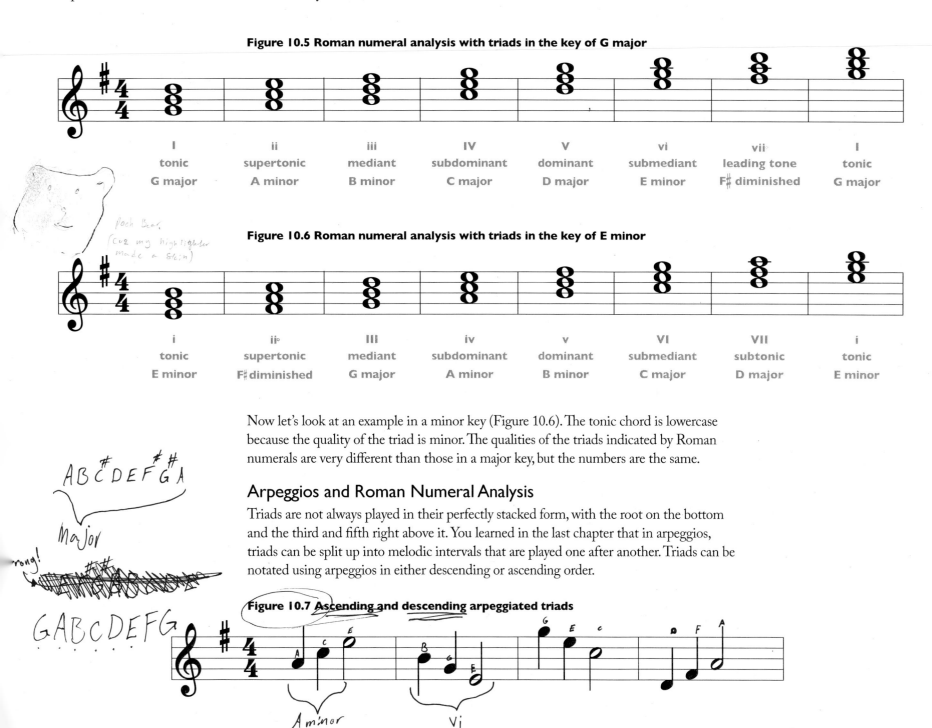

Figure 10.5 Roman numeral analysis with triads in the key of G major

I	ii	iii	IV	V	vi	vii°	I
tonic	supertonic	mediant	subdominant	dominant	submediant	leading tone	tonic
G major	A minor	B minor	C major	D major	E minor	F♯ diminished	G major

Figure 10.6 Roman numeral analysis with triads in the key of E minor

i	ii°	III	iv	v	VI	VII	i
tonic	supertonic	mediant	subdominant	dominant	submediant	subtonic	tonic
E minor	F♯ diminished	G major	A minor	B minor	C major	D major	E minor

Now let's look at an example in a minor key (Figure 10.6). The tonic chord is lowercase because the quality of the triad is minor. The qualities of the triads indicated by Roman numerals are very different than those in a major key, but the numbers are the same.

Arpeggios and Roman Numeral Analysis

Triads are not always played in their perfectly stacked form, with the root on the bottom and the third and fifth right above it. You learned in the last chapter that in arpeggios, triads can be split up into melodic intervals that are played one after another. Triads can be notated using arpeggios in either descending or ascending order.

Figure 10.7 Ascending and descending arpeggiated triads

how's an inverted triad **Activity 10.1—In-class activity**
different from a diatonic triad

GABC DEF#G

(DEF#GABC#D

Key sig.

#

A○

○

○

○ *dominant*

Major or minor =
the pattern of #s

Which four triads are being represented in the arpeggios notated in Figure 10.7? Get in groups of two to discover the triads expressed in the measures in Figure 10.7. Write your answers by giving the name of the triad (e.g., G major).

root = lowest sounding pitch

a) Measure 1 = ___*minor*___   b) Measure 2 = _____

c) Measure 3 = _____   d) Measure 4 = _____

Once you know the triad names and qualities of the notes, you can mark the analysis with Roman numerals.

First Measure: In the first measure is an A minor triad (A–C–E). By working to find the root of this triad, you are able to assess its relationship to the key and quality, and assign a Roman numeral.

The root of the chord is A, as an A–C–E configuration exists on all spaces, a defining characteristic of the triad. Since A is the root, you can discern its relationship to the key (G major), namely, that it is the supertonic triad, and quality, minor. In order to show both that this triad is minor and on the second degree of the scale, you write a lowercase Roman numeral ii.

Activity 10.2—In-class activity

Give the analysis with Roman numerals of the triads in Figure 10.7. Get in groups of two to discover the triads expressed in these measures. Write your answers with Roman numerals, including the correct capital or lowercase numeral indicating major or minor. Figure 10.7 is in the key of G major.

a) Measure 1 = ___*ii*___   b) Measure 2 = _____

c) Measure 3 = _____   d) Measure 4 = _____

85

Chapter 10 Review

Fill in the correct answers below. Hint: Write out the Roman numerals for the major
and minor scale to use as a reference as you complete this review.

_____ 1. ii

_____ 2. vi

_____ 3. III

_____ 4. V

_____ 5. iii

_____ 6. VI

_____ 7. IV

_____ 8. I

_____ 9. v

_____ 10. VII

_____ 11. vii°

_____ 12. ii°

_____ 13. i

_____ 14. iv

a. Submediant in major

b. Subdominant in minor

c. Mediant in major

d. Subtonic

e. Subdominant in major

f. Dominant in minor

g. Supertonic in minor

h. Supertonic in major

i. Submediant in minor

j. Mediant in minor

k. Leading tone

l. Tonic in minor

m. Tonic in major

n. Dominant in major

Daily Exercises for Chapter 10

EXERCISES FOR DAY 1

Exercise 10.1

Read through chapter 10 and answer the following questions:

a) What are diatonic triads?

b) Why is analysis with Roman numerals helpful?

c) Give an example of an arpeggiated triad below, including a key signature and a bass or treble clef.

Exercise 10.2

Label the triads below with the correct triad degrees, making sure to note the major key signatures.

a.

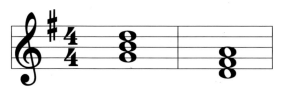

tonic _____   _____

b.

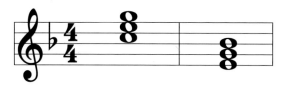

_____   _____

c.

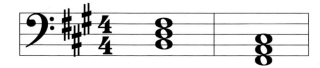

_____   _____

d.

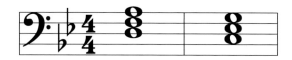

_____   _____

EXERCISES FOR DAY 2

Exercise 10.3

Give the corresponding Roman numeral, including quality, for the triad degrees below.

Major Key

a) supertonic: ___*ii*___ b) dominant: _____ c) submediant: _____

d) leading tone: _____ e) mediant: _____ f) subdominant: _____

Minor Key

a) supertonic: ___*ii°*___ b) dominant: _____ c) submediant: _____

d) subtonic: _____ e) mediant: _____ f) subdominant: _____

Exercise 10.4

Use Roman numerals to identify the triads in the indicated **major** keys.

a.

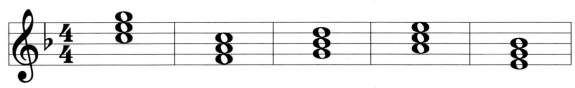

F major   *V* _____ _____ _____ _____

b.

E major _____ _____ _____ _____ _____

c.

E♭ major _____   _____   _____   _____   _____

d.

D major _____   _____   _____   _____   _____

EXERCISES FOR DAY 3

Exercise 10.5

Use Roman numerals to identify the triads in the indicated **minor** keys.

a.

D minor   *VII* _____   _____   _____   _____

b.

B minor _____   _____   _____   _____   _____

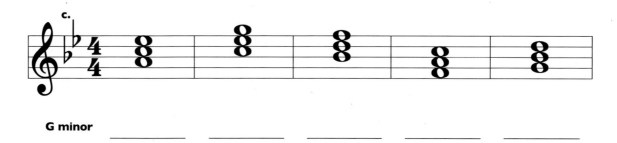

G minor _____ _____ _____ _____

Exercise 10.6

Give Roman numeral analysis to the arpeggiated triads below. The keys are all **major** keys.

iii _____ _____ _____ _____

_____ _____ _____ _____

c.

EXERCISES FOR DAY 4

Exercise 10.7

    a) Label the triads below by letter and quality.

    b) Label the triads below by triad degree name.

    c) Label the triads in Roman numeral analysis.

    d) Transpose the triads to the key of F major. Hint: Follow the steps for transposing
        from chapter 7. Remember that Roman numeral analysis communicates the scale
        degree number.

D major _____ _____ _____ _____ _____

tonic _____ _____ _____ _____ _____

I _____ _____ _____ _____ _____

Triad Inversions

Most music is not written in a series of perfectly stacked triads. Very often the notes are rearranged, played in succession, or stacked differently. Up until now you have learned triads in root position because this is their simplest form, but in this chapter, you will learn how to identify and create inversions for the triad qualities discussed in chapter 10 as well as analyze the chords with Roman numerals.

There are two different inversions for any triad, depending on the bottom note. In this chapter you will learn these two inversions and how to identify, notate, and analyze them in a variety of situations.

In identifying types of triad inversions, you are using what you have learned in chapters 1–10. In these last few chapters, we are approaching the goal and culmination of this book. Stay focused and determined as we near the finish line!

Introduction to Inverted Triads: Root Position

An **inverted triad** occurs when the notes are rearranged so that the root is no longer the lowest sounding pitch. Recall that a triad is a three-note chord written in thirds consisting of the root, third, and fifth. If the three notes of the triad are placed in a different order so that the root is no longer the lowest note, the chord is now in an inversion.

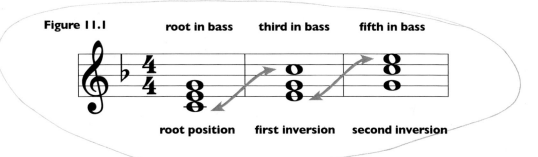

Figure 11.1

root in bass   third in bass   fifth in bass

root position   first inversion   second inversion

BONUS

root position   root is lowest
first inversion   third is lowest
second inversion   fifth is lowest

When the root of the triad is the lowest sounding pitch, or acting **bass note**, the triad is in **root position**. When the third of the triad is lowest, the triad is in **first inversion**. When the fifth of the triad is the lowest, the triad is in **second inversion**.

inverted triad = root is no longer the lowest sounding note

In order to properly invert triads, you must be careful to know the notes of the triad before you invert it since the notes of a triad do not change, no matter what form it is in.

Figure 11.2

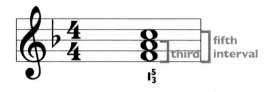

A triad can be named with the method of analysis you learned in chapter 10. The numbers $\frac{5}{3}$ may be placed next to the Roman numeral to denote a root position chord. The reason for the number 5 is because the distance from the bottom note to the top note is a fifth interval in size. The reason for the number 3 is because the distance from the bottom note to the middle note is a third interval in size.

First Inversion Triads

In a first inversion triad, the third is the lowest-sounding pitch. When written on one staff, the root is moved up an octave, leaving the third as the lowest note.

Figure 11.3   **first inversion** *= brings it up one octave*

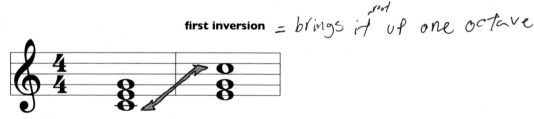

In this example, the bottom note of the root position C triad has been raised a full octave. In Figure 11.4 on the next page, the first inversion is symbolized by the number 6 placed to the right of the Roman numeral. The number 6 is used because the distance from the bass (E) to the top note (C) is a sixth interval in size.

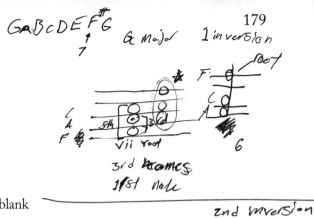

Figure 11.4

sixth
interval

I⁶

Activity 11.1—In-class activity

Make the following root position triads into first inversion triads in the blank
measures on the right. Include the Roman numeral and inversion number.

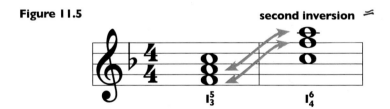

iii⁵₃   iii⁶   IV⁵₃   IV⁵₃   ii⁵₃

basic

Second Inversion Triads

In a second inversion triad, the fifth is the lowest sounding pitch. When written on one
staff, both the root and third of the chord are transposed up an octave, leaving the fifth as
the lowest note.

Figure 11.5

second inversion

I⁵₃   I⁶₄

Notice in this example how the root and third of the F triad have been raised a full octave.
In Roman numeral analysis of a second inversion triad, the numbers 6 and 4 are placed to
the right of the Roman numeral because the distance from the bass (C) to the top note
(A) is an interval of a sixth and the distance from the bass (C) to the middle note (F) is an
interval of a fourth.

Figure 11.6

Activity 11.2—In-class activity

Change the following root position triads into first and second inversion triads in the blank measures on the right. Include the Roman numeral and inversion number(s) on each triad.

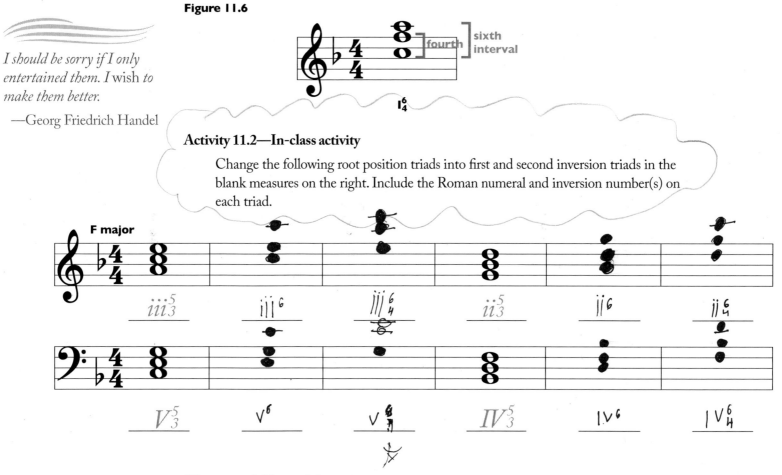

Close and Open Harmony

As you might be able to tell, inversions do not always look as neat and precise as the root position. First and second inversions seem to break apart the neatly stacked triad; however, in all the variations you've seen so far, the notes of the triad are as close as possible to the bottom note. This is called **close harmony**. The notes of a chord can also be spread more than an octave, referred to as **open harmony**.

Close Harmony

For example, notice in Figure 11.7 how the notes G, B, and D of the G major triad are organized as close as possible to the bottom note in both the root and the inversions.

Figure 11.7

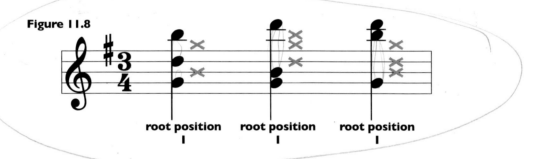

root position   first inversion   second inversion

Open Harmony

These notes can also be spaced farther apart, in a more open harmony. In open harmony, the notes of the triad are spaced over more than an octave. To continue with the G major triad, notice how in the examples below, although all three triads have G, B, and D in them, the notes are spaced farther apart so that other notes in the triad *could* be placed in-between, but are not.

Figure 11.8

root position   root position   root position
I   I   I

Because the notes do not change—there is a G, B, and D in all three examples—they are all G major triads, and moreover, because they all have G as the lowest sounding pitch, they are all root position triads. The note at the bottom is the deciding factor in determining the inversion of a triad, regardless of the order of the notes above it.

The following chords in Figure 11.9 are examples of open and close harmonies.

close

open

Figure 11.9

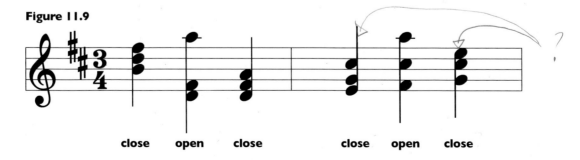

close   open   close   close   open   close

Chapter 11 Review

Word List

DGB	**CFA**
DFA	**EGC**
FIRST	**GBE**
ROOT	**SECOND**

1 Position where the root of the triad is in the bass

2 Inversion where the third of the triad is in the bass

3 Inversion where the fifth of the triad is in the bass

4 Notes in order of C major triad first inversion

5 Notes in order of F major triad second inversion

6 Notes in order of D minor triad root position

7 Notes in order of E minor triad first inversion

8 Notes in order of G major triad second inversion

Daily Exercises for Chapter 11

In these exercises for working with inversions, there will be no minor keys. All of the examples in your exercises will be major key signatures.

EXERCISES FOR DAY 1

Exercise 11.1

Rewrite the root position triads below into first and second inversion triads.

a.

b.

c.
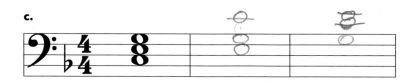

d.

Rewrite the second inversion triads into root position triads.

a.
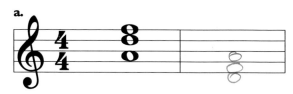

b.

Exercise 11.2

Identify the following triads as root, first, or second inversions.

root   first   first   second   first   root   second

first   root   second   root   second   second   first

🎼 EXERCISES FOR DAY 2

Exercise 11.3

a) Label the triads below by letter and quality.

b) Label the triads below by triad degree name.

c) Label the triads in Roman numeral analysis including inversion type.

d) Transpose the triads into the key of D major. Hint: Follow the steps for transposing from chapter 7. Remember that Roman numeral analysis communicates the scale degree number.

a) D minor | D minor | D minor | A dim | F Major | C minor | Bb Major

b) mediant | mediant | mediant | leading tone | dominant | Super tonic | tonic

c) iii$^5_3$ | iii$^6_4$ | iii^6 | vii$^{o5}_3$ | V^6 | ii^6 | I$^5_3$

Exercise 11.4

Label the following triads with Roman numeral analysis, indicating the type of inversion. Make sure you note the key signatures. Both are major keys.

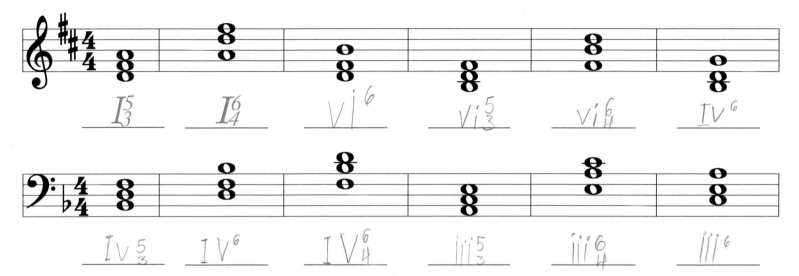

ᢙ EXERCISES FOR DAY 3

Exercise 11.5

Rewrite the following augmented and diminished triads into first and second inversions.

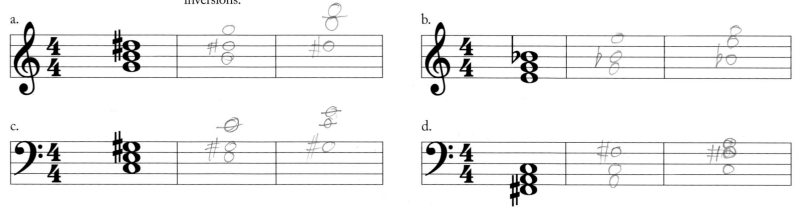

Label the following augmented or diminished triads below as either root, first inversion, or second inversion.

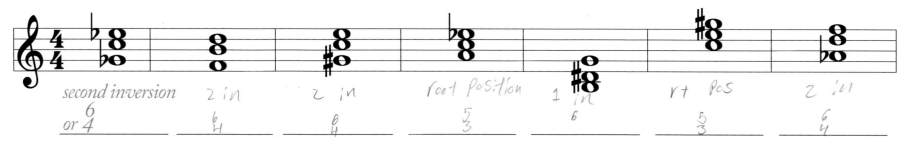

second inversion   2 in   2 in   root Position   1 in   rt Pos   2 in
6   6   6   5   6   5   6
or 4   4   4   3   3   4

Exercise 11.6

Finish writing the triads indicated by the Roman numeral analysis. The given note is the lowest-sounding pitch. Assume each staff is in a major key (not minor). Add sharps or flats as needed to form the indicated triads.

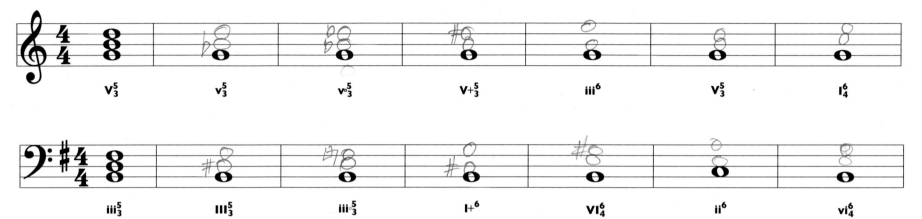

✦ EXERCISES FOR DAY 4

Exercise 11.7

Label the following triads with Roman numeral analysis, indicating the type of inversion. Make sure you note the key signature. Assume each staff is in a major key.

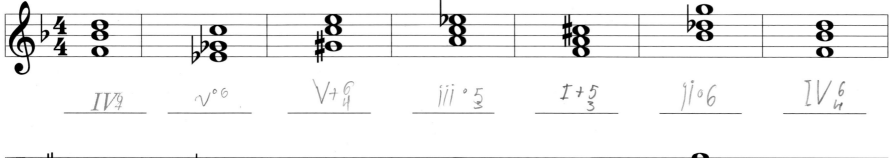

$IV\frac{7}{}$ $v°6$ $V+\frac{6}{4}$ $iii°\frac{}{3}$ $I+\frac{5}{3}$ $ii°6$ $IV\frac{6}{4}$

V^6 $iii°\frac{5}{3}$ $I\frac{5}{3}$ $I+6$ $IV+°$ $vii°\frac{6}{4}$ IV^6

Exercise 11.8 Advanced Theory (Brain Teasers)

Build the specified triad above the given bass note. If the note does not contain an accidental, it is meant to be natural. The key signatures are not given or needed. The types of inversions will indicate all you need to give the correct triad and quality. If there are no inversion number(s), it is a root position. Do not be impatient; this exercise will take you some time. Use your keyboard sheet if needed. Write the name of each triad above the notated triad as noted in the examples below.

Aug = augmented   dim = diminished   m = minor   M = major

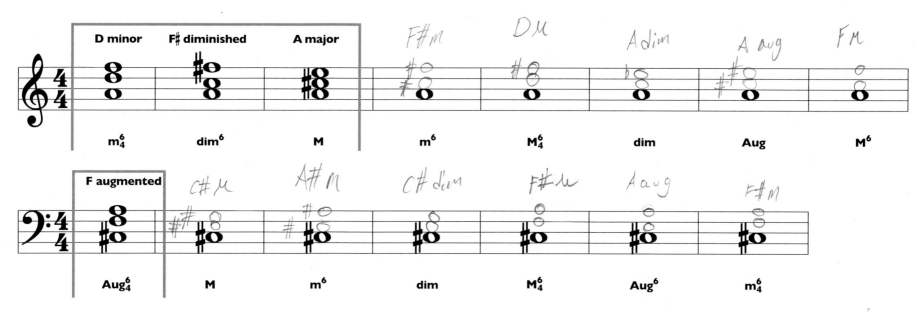

12 Score Analysis

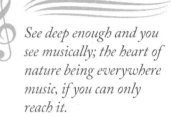

See deep enough and you see musically; the heart of nature being everywhere music, if you can only reach it.

—Thomas Carlyle

In this chapter you arrive at the culmination of this course: learning to analyze whole scores of music in order to understand the basics of harmonic structure and reasoning behind compositions.

As you have already seen in chapter 11, triads can be inverted and arranged so that the notes are spread out over larger areas (open and closed harmony). Part of triad analysis includes an analysis of the notes in both the treble and bass clefs. Most of your analysis has either been from the treble or the bass clefs. In this chapter, you will learn to interact with triads in a score by analyzing the notes in both the treble and bass clefs.

You have worked with triads that consist mostly of three notes. Do not be intimidated by an analysis of a chord or group of notes containing more than three notes. You will learn how to approach "extra" notes that may be included in the chords. These notes are often not needed to properly assign a Roman numeral to the chord. You will also learn how to recognize "implied" notes.

There are a few chords within your scores that go beyond the scope of this course. This should not give you cause for alarm as you will see how to make sense of these chords. The score analysis in this chapter will consist primarily of triads you have already learned.

Triads Using Both Clefs

Triads, of course, can stretch across both the treble and bass staff in a score. When you analyze a score, you are analyzing the whole vertical stack from the bass to the treble.

The measures in Figure 12.1 are part of the beginning score of the hymn "When Peace Like a River." On the following page is numbered commentary on specific chords.

Figure 12.1

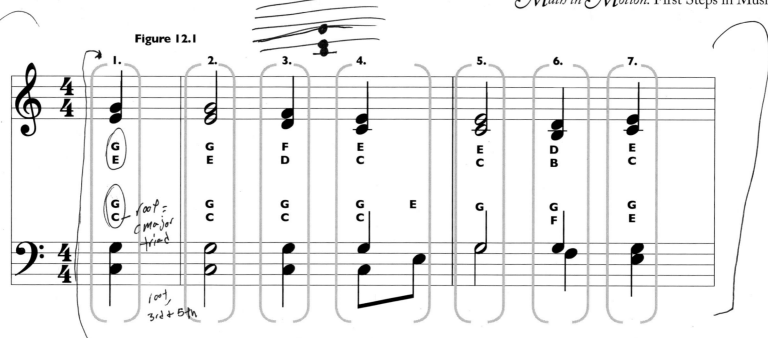

Group 1: Taking all of the notes notated for both clefs on the first beat, you have G, E, G, and C. Through your analysis, you can reduce this by counting repeated notes once as they are the same pitch and do not change the chord. You now have G, E, and C. If you arrange these notes on a staff, you will find a stack of lines or spaces in which C is the bottom note, and thus the root. Therefore, you have a C major triad, as C is the root and the third and fifth are major and perfect, respectively.

Below the bass clef, you can put a capital Roman numeral I_3^5, since the key signature is C and the tonic triad is the C major triad. See Figure 12.2 on the following page.

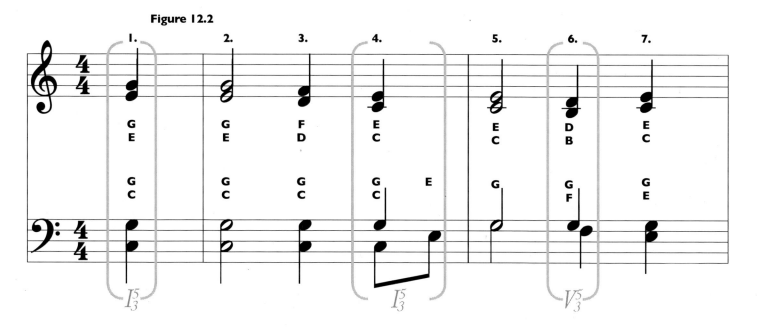

Figure 12.2

Group 4: On the fourth beat, taking all the notes from both the treble and bass clefs, you have E, C, G, C, and E. The two eighth notes are incorporated into the analysis because they are both played with the other quarter notes. Since an eighth note is half of a quarter note, both eighth notes mix into the chord and must be incorporated into the analysis. Once you reduce the duplicate notes, you have C, E, G—once again, the C major triad, or capital Roman numeral I_3^5.

The "Extra" Notes

When you are analyzing a score and labeling triads, sometimes the score will include chords with more notes than the three notes of a triad. Many times these "extra" notes make up larger chords that you have not learned in this curriculum, but all these chords are simply extensions of triads. An example of this kind of chord is in number 6 of Figure 12.2, which is called a **seventh chord**. A seventh chord is comprised of a triad (root–third–fifth) plus an additional note, seventh above the root. If you wish to learn more about seventh chords, please see the Supplemental Material section.

Group 6: In this group, you have D, B, G, and F notes from both clefs. There are four different notes, no duplicates. If you look for a triad, you should be able to identify G, B, and D with G as a root, and B, D, F with B as a root. Since both of these readings cannot be correct, you should attempt to find to find an order of notes in which all four pitches are on lines or spaces. In so doing you will form a chord of four notes: the root, the third, the fifth, and the seventh. The seventh, F, in this example, is the "extra" note and goes into the realm of seventh chords. In your score analysis, for now, ignore the "extra" note (F) and label the chord as capital Roman numeral V for the G major triad.

Using the "Implied" Notes

Score analysis often involves analyzing chords that are somewhat incomplete. For instance, a piece might include a C major chord made up of only a C and G, with the E missing. In this case, the E is implied. The one note of a chord that cannot be implied, however, is the root, leading to the following rule:

Rule: **Never label a group of notes as a specific triad if the root is not in the group of notes being analyzed**.

It takes a bit of practice to know when a note is implied and when it is not. Look at the examples below to see how different notes can be implied in triads.

Figure 12.3   **Figure 12.4**

In the example shown in Figure 12.3, the C and E are included in two different triads—the C major triad and the A minor triad. Remember, however, that the root of a chord cannot be left out, and since there is no A in this example, it cannot be A minor. You can therefore conclude that it is a C major triad.

In the example seen in Figure 12.4, you must pay attention to the key signature. Here you have a C and G, suggesting perhaps that an E is implied. But since the key signature is the key of B♭, the E would be flatted. With a C, E♭, and G, you can conclude that it is a C minor triad.

Activity 12.1—In-class activity

Use the "implied" notes for each pair of notes below by labeling the notes with the correct type of triad. Note the key differences in each measure.

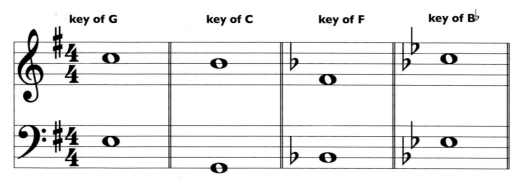

Triad: _____ _____ _____ _____

Analysis Continued…

When you analyze a score, you are essentially untangling a set of notes to correctly label their harmonies and their relationships to the tonic or key. The purpose of analysis is to distinguish the harmonic foundation from the other complexities of a composition.

The excerpt in Figure 12.5 is the beginning of the "Old Hundredth (Doxology)." Using your knowledge of triads, look at how these notes are decrypted correctly into triad names.

Figure 12.5

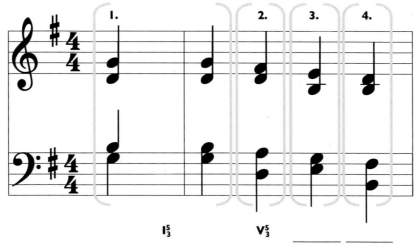

Music . . . can name the unnameable and communicate the unknowable.

—Leonard Bernstein

Group 1: In the first two stacks of notes, the chords are exactly the same; therefore, both sets are considered as one triad. The notes contained are G, B, D, and G. By counting the duplicate note once, you now have G, B, and D. When you arrange the notes on a staff, you discover that the root is G and that these notes make up the G major triad.

Since the key is G major, put a Roman numeral I_3^5.

Group 2: This group of notes contains the following notes: D, A, D, and F♯. By counting the duplicate note once, you have D, A, and F♯. By arranging these notes on a staff, you find that D is the root and that the notes make up the D major triad. Since the D major triad is in the key of G major, for your analysis put a Roman numeral V_3^5 below the staff.

Activity 12.2—In-class activity

Finish analyzing the excerpt in Figure 12.5 by labeling groups 3 and 4 with the correct Roman numeral analysis. Students may work in groups of two.

Group 3: notes in group _____ _____ _____ _____

triad name _____

Roman numeral in key of G _____

Group 4: notes in group _____ _____ _____ _____

triad name _____

Roman numeral in key of G _____

Inversions in Analysis

As you learned in chapter 11, triads can be arranged so that the root is not the lowest sounding pitch. These inversions, as they are called, are notated with the number [6] and [6][4] next to the Roman numeral. [6] denotes first inversion where the third of the chord is the lowest sounding pitch, and [6][4] denotes second inversion where the fifth is the lowest sounding pitch.

Figure 12.6

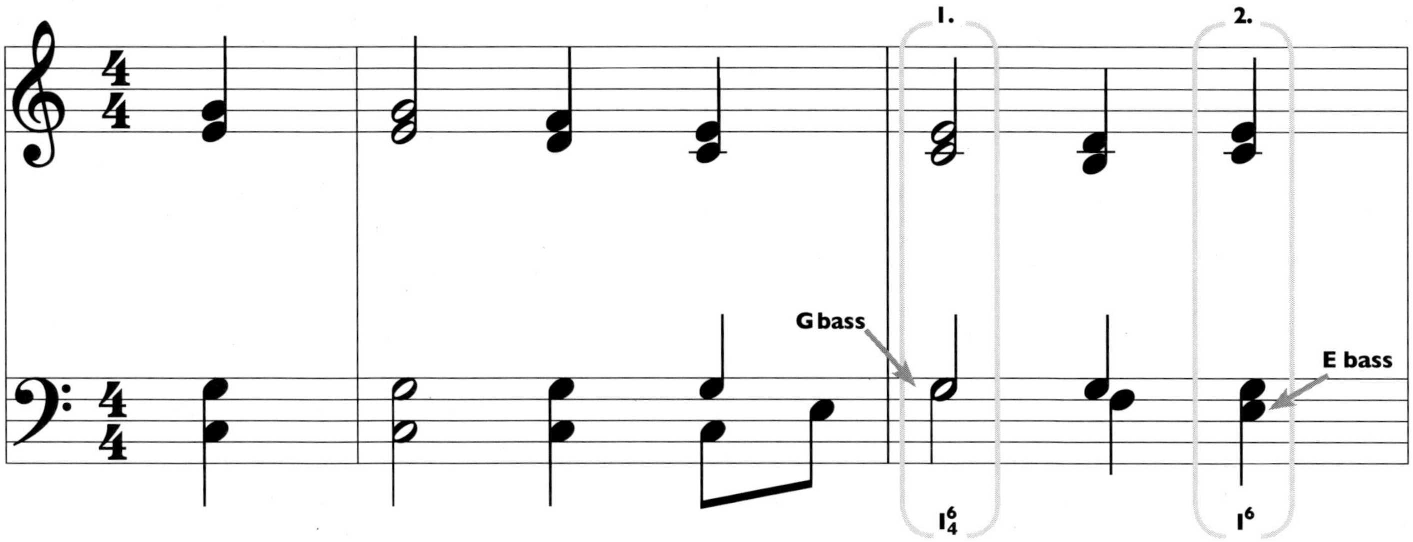

Group 1: This group contains the following notes: E, C, and G. You know these notes make up the C major triad. You should remember from the previous chapter to use the lowest note of the chord to determine the type of inversion. The lowest note in this group of notes is the G. In the C major triad, the G note is the fifth in the triad. Using your knowledge of inversions, second inversion is the type of inversion with the fifth note of the triad in the bass. Second inversion is labeled with a $^6_4$ to the right of the Roman numeral.

Group 2: Notes E, C, G, and E also make up the C major triad once duplicates are counted once. What is the lowest note in this group? With the E as the lowest-sounding pitch, you know this to be the third of the C major triad. Since the third is the lowest-sounding pitch, you know to put a ^{6} to the right of the Roman numeral, indicating first inversion.

Inversions are always identified by looking at the lowest note of a group of notes you are analyzing. It is always done with Roman numerals and will always include an analysis of both the treble and bass clefs.

Activity 12.3—In-class activity

Excerpt from "There Is a Fountain"

Finish labeling the Roman numerals below with the correct inversion type.

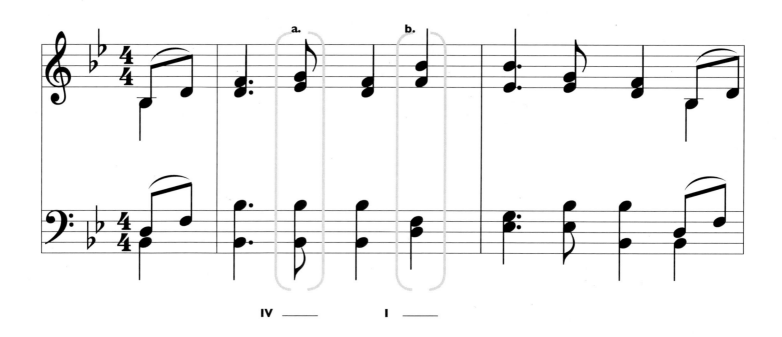

IV ——   I ——

Musical Symbols on the Staff

As you begin to examine musical scores more closely, you will notice that they contain many symbols that we have not yet discussed. Identifying symbols on the staff is just like reading a sentence in a book or a math equation, except that you use different symbols to express your meaning. Take a minute to look at the following staff, and then go on to read the definition of each symbol.

Figure 12.7

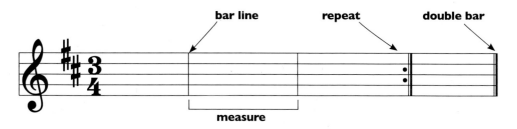

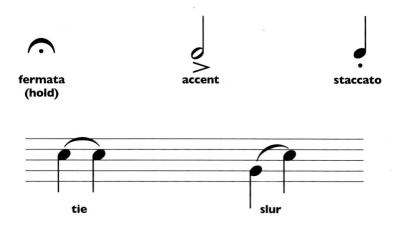

BONUS

The difference between a tie and a slur is that a tie connects two notes of the same pitch, and a slur connects notes of different pitches.

Functions of Symbols on the Staff

repeat. A symbol (:‖) used to signify that the musician should repeat the musical phrase immediately before the repeat sign.

double bar. A line showing that the piece is over or that there is a major shift in the overall idea of the piece, such as a key or time signature change.

fermata. A symbol (⌢) used to show the note should be held longer than the normal note value. The duration is usually up to the musician's discretion.

accent mark. A stress or emphasis placed on the note.

staccato. Detached, separated; denoting a style in which the tones played are more abruptly disconnected.

tie. A curved line connecting two notes of the same pitch that are to be sounded as one note equal to their combined note value.

slur. A curved line between two different notes indicating the notes are connected and should be played smoothly.

Now that you know what these symbols mean, try to identify them in the hymn scores and other music that you see.

Chapters 6–12 Review

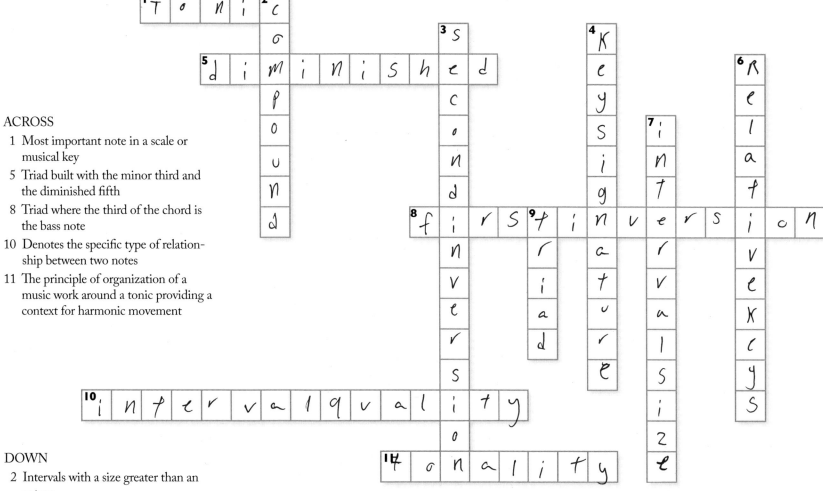

ACROSS

1 Most important note in a scale or musical key

5 Triad built with the minor third and the diminished fifth

8 Triad where the third of the chord is the bass note

10 Denotes the specific type of relationship between two notes

11 The principle of organization of a music work around a tonic providing a context for harmonic movement

DOWN

2 Intervals with a size greater than an octave

3 Triad where the fifth of the chord is the bass note

4 Indicates the key of the piece at the beginning of the staff by showing which sharps or flats are to be used

6 Pairs of major and minor scales that share the same key signature

7 The distance between two notes that is found by counting lines and spaces, or letter names, represented on the staff

9 Formed with three notes consisting of the root, the third from the root, and the fifth from the root

Daily Exercises for Chapter 12

EXERCISES FOR DAY 1

Exercise 12.1

Use both the bass and treble clefs to analyze the type of triad in the scores below (but do not yet write out the inversion). Write out the notes.

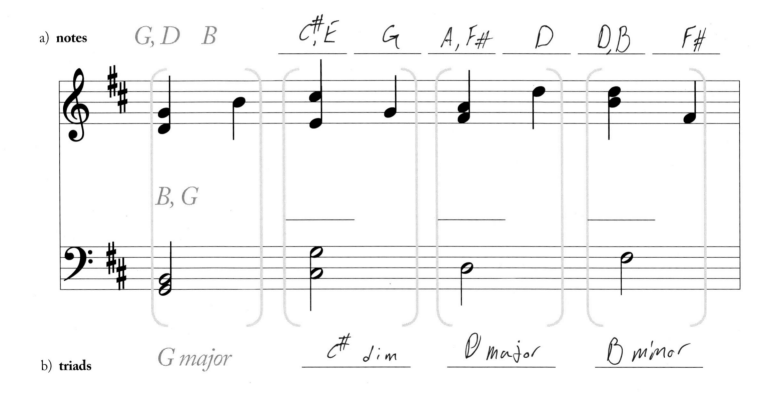

Exercise 12.2

Use the notes below to identify the type of triad in each group of notes (e.g., G major). Inversion should not be given.

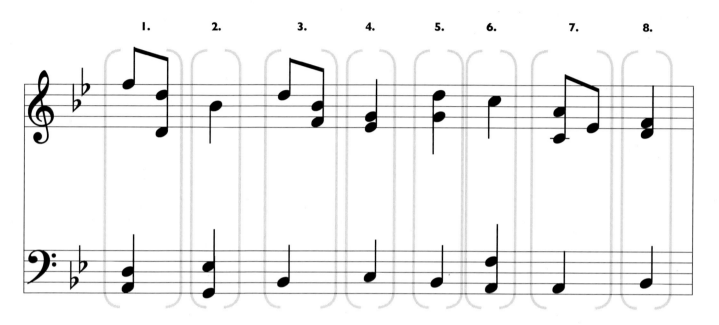

1.   D minor   2.   E♭ major

3.   B♭ major   4.   C minor

5.   G minor   6.   F major

7.   A diminished   8.   B♭ major

EXERCISES FOR DAY 2

Exercise 12.3

Label the type of triad in each group of notes below. Each group of notes contains "extra" notes. Circle the "extra" note and list it next to the triad name. The first one has been completed for you.

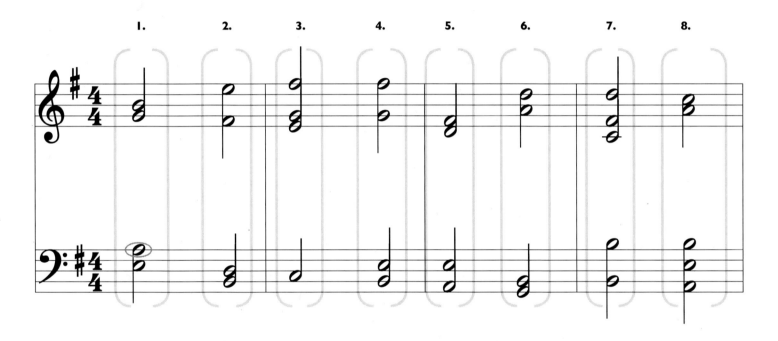

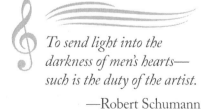

To send light into the darkness of men's hearts— such is the duty of the artist.

—Robert Schumann

1. *E minor, A*

2. B minor, E

3. C major, F#

4. E minor, F#

5. D major, E

6. G major, A

7. B minor, C

8. A minor, B

Exercise 12.4

Label the type of triad in each group of notes below. Note that all of these groups of notes have implied notes. Mark the position of the "implied" note(s) with an "x" and list it next to the triad name.

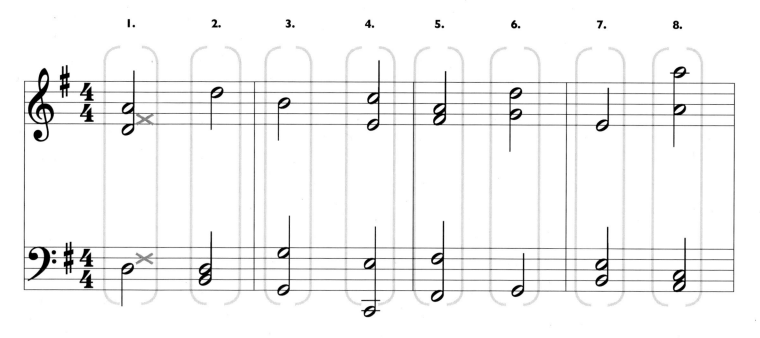

1. _D major, F♯_

2. B minor, F♯

3. G Major D

4. C Major, G

5. F♯ dimininished C

6. G major, B

7. E minor G

8. A minor, E

🎼 EXERCISES FOR DAY 3

Exercise 12.5

Use Roman numerals and inversion numbers in your analysis of the groups of notes indicated below in this excerpt from "When I Survey the Wondrous Cross." The lowest note in each group of notes will help you determine the inversion type.

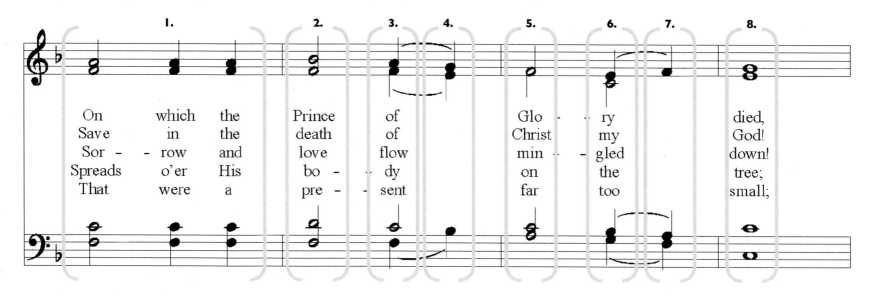

1. ___ I $^5_3$ ___   2. ___ V $^6_4$ ___   3. ___ I $^5_3$ ___

4. ___ vii° $^6_4$ or V $^5_3$ ___   5. ___ I ^{6} ___   6. ___ V $^6_4$ ___

7. ___ I $^5_3$ ___   8. ___ V $^5_3$ ___

Exercise 12.6

Use Roman numerals and inversion numbers in your analysis for the groups of notes indicated below in this excerpt from "There Is a Fountain."

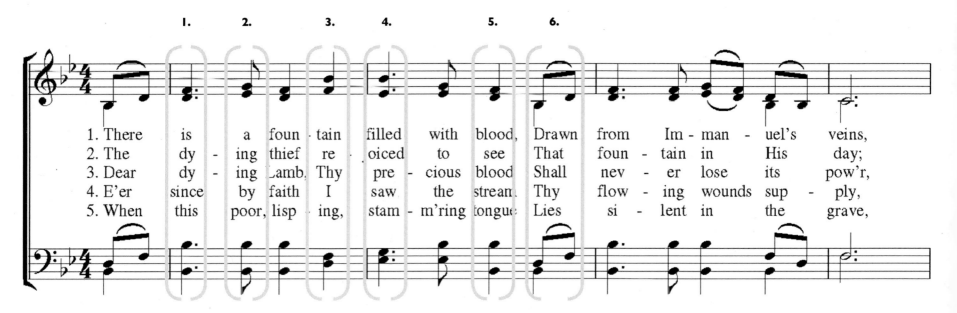

1. _____ $I\frac{5}{3}$ _____ 2. _____ $IV\frac{6}{4}$ _____ 3. _____ I^6 _____

4. _____ $IV\frac{5}{3}$ _____ 5. _____ $I\frac{5}{3}$ _____ 6. _____ $I\frac{5}{3}$ _____

❦ EXERCISES FOR DAY 4

Exercise 12.7

Transpose the excerpt from "When I Survey the Wondrous Cross" below into the key of D major. You may want to transfer the Roman numerals from Day 3 Exercise 12.5 to this page before beginning. Hint: Follow the steps for transposing from chapter 7. Remember that Roman numeral analysis communicates the scale degree number.

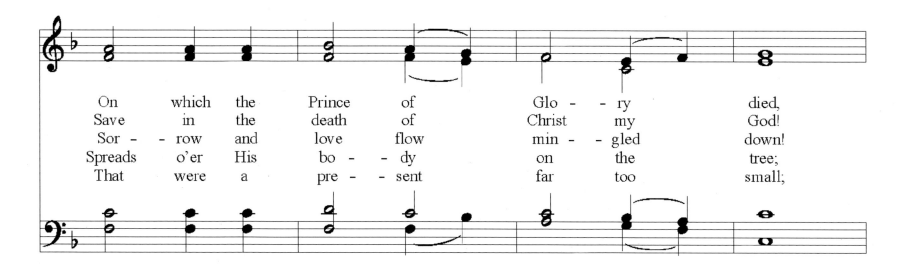

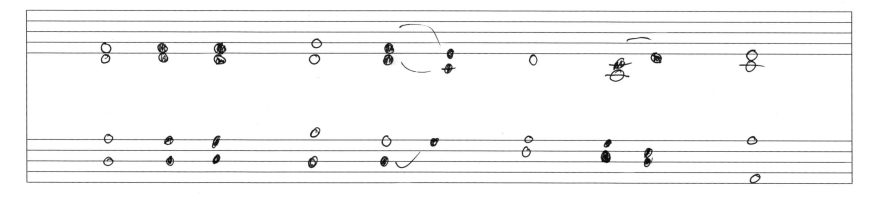

13 Review

Congratulations! In the past twelve chapters, you have gotten through a lot of information. Do not be discouraged if you have not grasped all of the material perfectly; it can take time to fully master the details of some of the concepts introduced. If you enjoyed what you learned here, there is a whole world to explore that far surpasses the range and scope of this book.

In this final chapter, you will review several important aspects of the music theory concepts we have discussed. This chapter should help you solidify many concepts and give you a chance to rediscover elements you may have forgotten.

Pitch

All music can be reduced to two basic elements:

1. pitch—the attribute of a musical tone produced by the number of vibrations generating it, and

2. rhythm—the passage of pitch through time.

When we discussed pitch, we learned that there are seven different letter names used to represent different pitches: A, B, C, D, E, F, and G. Furthermore, we learned that these seven pitches can be adjusted a half step higher or lower through the use of sharps, flats, and naturals.

To express pitch in written form, we use a staff with a clef.

treble clef: a symbol used to notate pitches that are to be played with the right hand or a higher pitched instrument. This is also called the G clef because this symbol evolved from the letter G. Its curve always encircles the line for the G note.

BONUS

half step *(n.)* **the shortest distance between two notes**

[Music is] an agreeable harmony for the honor of God and the permissible delights of the soul.

—Johann Sebastian Bach

 **bass clef**: a symbol used to notate pitches that are to be played with the left hand or a lower pitched instrument. This is also called the F clef because this symbol evolved from the letter F. The two dots always surround the line for the F note.

Once we know the note name of a given line or space, we can extrapolate all of the remaining lines and spaces.

If you feel that you need a bit more review of pitch and how to notate it, read chapter 1 and review the exercises.

Rhythm

Rhythm, the second basic element of music, is understood as the passage of pitch through time. To express this, we use several notes: the whole note, the half note, the quarter note, the eighth note, and the sixteenth note. As the diagram below illustrates, these notes have a level of hierarchy. The whole note has the greatest value, the half note is half the value of the whole note, and the quarter note is half the value of the half note. This process of division continues as we work down to smaller note values.

Figure 13.1

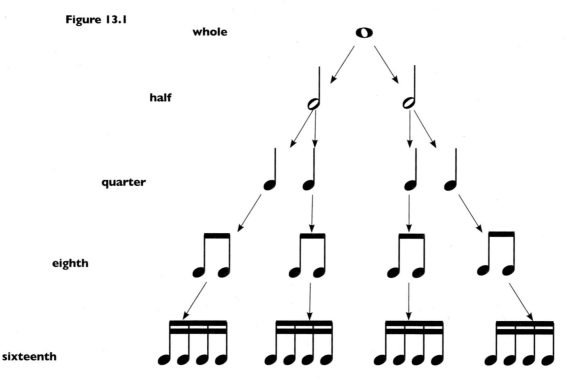

If you feel that you need a bit more review of the basics of rhythm, read chapter 2 and review the exercises.

Simple and Compound Meter

To be able to combine pitches and rhythms to create music, we use meter. **Meter** describes the specific beat groupings and divisions that occur within music. Recall that the **beat** is the fixed, rhythmic pulse of the piece of music.

There are two types of meter: simple and compound. **Simple meter** is defined as a meter in which the beat is divided into two equal parts. **Compound meter** is defined as a meter in which the beat is divided into three equal parts.

These meters are expressed through **time signatures**: a vertical stack of numbers placed at the beginning of the staff immediately following the clef to indicate the meter (Figure 13.2).

Figure 13.2

We can quickly assess the type of meter being expressed through a given time signature by looking at the top number. When the top number is 2, 3, or 4, the time signature it represents is simple meter. When the top number is 6, 9, or 12, the time signature it represents is compound meter.

Top Number of Time Signature	Meter Type	Number of Beat Divisions
2	simple	two
3	simple	two
4	simple	two
6	compound	three
9	compound	three
12	compound	three

A time signature that represents simple meter gives two important pieces of information. The top number gives the number of beats per measure and the bottom number gives the type of note that receives the beat. In the example below, the top number is 2. Since the time signature represents simple meter, there are two beats in each measure. The bottom number is 2, meaning the half note receives the beat.

Figure 13.3

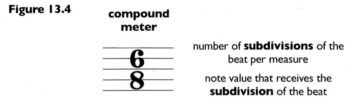

A time signature that represents compound meter also gives the musician two pieces of important information. The top number gives the number of *subdivisions* of the beat per measure, while the bottom number gives the type of note that receives the subdivision. In the example below, the top number is 6, meaning that there are six subdivisions in each measure. The bottom number is 8, meaning that the eighth note receives the subdivision.

Figure 13.4

To find the value of the beat, multiply the subdivision of the beat (the eighth note) by three. In so doing, we find out that the beat value is a dotted quarter note.

Figure 13.5

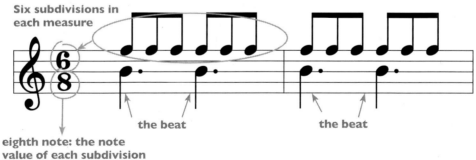

If you feel that you need a bit more review of the simple and compound meter, read chapters 3 and 4 and review the exercises.

Scales and Key Signatures

A **scale** is a series of musical notes organized by ascending or descending pitches. There are two basic types of scales discussed in this book: major and natural minor. These scales are built upon patterns of half steps and whole steps. The pattern for a major scale is W–W–H–W–W–W–H.

Figure 13.6   **C Major Scale**

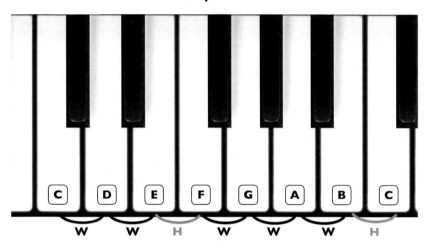

You can pick any starting note and build a major scale using the given pattern.

The pattern for a natural minor scale is W–H–W–W–H–W–W.

Figure 13.7   **A Natural Minor Scale**

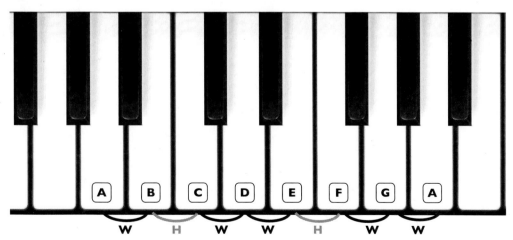

You can pick any starting note and create a natural minor scale as long as you use this pattern.

Scales serve as foundations for key signatures, as key signatures are established and derived from scales. Suppose we apply the pattern of half steps and whole steps for a major scale to the starting note G. In doing this, we create a G major scale with the notes G, A, B, C, D, E, F♯, and G. We can extract the sharp in this scale, and place it at the beginning of the staff to create a key signature with one sharp: F♯.

Figure 13.8   **G major scale**

When writing key signatures, the sharps or flats always appear in a specific order. The order of sharps is F–C–G–D–A–E–B. The order of flats is B–E–A–D–G–C–F.

To identify a given key signature, there are two main methods. In key signatures with sharps, the major key is a half step up from the last sharp. For example, if you are given a key signature with three sharps, F♯, C♯, and G♯, you simply go to the last sharp, G♯, and move a half step higher to A. Therefore, a key signature with three sharps represents the key of A major.

Figure 13.9

In key signatures with flats, the second to last flat is always the name of the major key. In the example below there are five flats: B♭, E♭, A♭, D♭, and G♭. The second to last flat is a D♭ meaning that the key is D♭ major.

Figure 13.10

In addition to major and natural minor scales and key signatures, we also discussed relative keys and scales. To review this concept, and others relating to scales and key signatures, read chapters 5 and 6 and review the daily exercises, or take a look at the Circle of Fifths.

Transposition

Transposition is the process of rewriting notes at a higher or lower pitch level. This process involves a change in key signature and pitch, but not in time signature or rhythm. To complete this process it is helpful to understand that each note in a scale has a scale degree number and a scale degree name.

Scale Degree Number	Scale Degree Name	Meaning
$\hat{1}$	tonic	most important note; the tonal center
$\hat{2}$	supertonic	above ("super") the tonic
$\hat{3}$	mediant	middle note between tonic and dominant
$\hat{4}$	subdominant	below ("sub") the dominant
$\hat{5}$	dominant	second-most important note
$\hat{6}$	submediant	lower mediant (between dominant and tonic)
$\hat{7}$	leading tone	strong pull ("leads") to the tonic
$\hat{1}$	tonic	upper tonic—the tonal center, an octave higher

Scale degree numbers and scale degree names stay the same in natural minor scales with only one exception. In a natural minor scale, the scale degree number $\hat{7}$ is called the **subtonic**, and is a whole step down from the octave tonic. With this in mind, we can look at transposition. When transposing melodies, there are five basic steps:

1) Know the key of the given melody.

2) Write the scale degree numbers of each note of the given melody.

3) Know the key into which you are transposing and write the key signature.

4) Transfer the scale degree numbers to the new melody.

5) Write the notes of the new melody. It is generally best to write notes that are in the same octave as the original piece.

To see these steps in progress, review chapter 7.

Intervals

An **interval** is the distance between two notes or two pitches. There are two parts to each interval: size and quality. The size of the interval is simply the number of lines and spaces between the two notes. Starting with the first note as one and counting upward, we can find the size of any interval. The size of the interval below is a fifth, as there are five lines and spaces when starting on the D and counting up to the A.

Figure 13.11

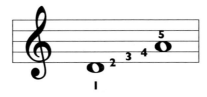

There are categories of intervals relating to quality: natural intervals and adjusted intervals. An interval is natural when the top note is part of the key or major scale of the lowest note. An interval is adjusted when the top note is not part of the key or major scale of the lowest note.

When an interval is natural, the interval is either major or perfect depending on the interval size. See below.

Interval Sizes		Natural Interval Quality
2nd, 3rd, 6th, 7th	are	major
unison, 4th, 5th, 8*va*	are	perfect

When an interval is adjusted, it is raised or lowered outside the key or scale of the lowest note. We discuss the raising and lowering of notes in terms of half steps. The chart on the next page demonstrates how the qualities change when the notes are raised and lowered.

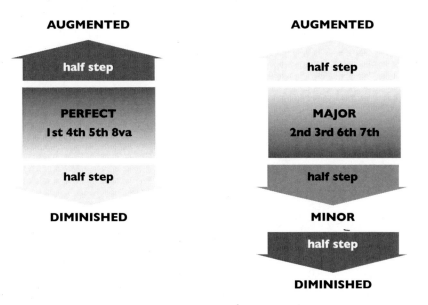

The discussion of intervals in chapter 8 is in detail. It would be wise to read that chapter again, as it serves as a foundation for chapters 9, 10, 11, and 12.

Triad Qualities

A triad is the simplest chord and is so named because it is formed with three notes: the root, third, and fifth. There are four types of triads: major, minor, diminished, and augmented. The types of triads, known as triad qualities, are created by combining different patterns of thirds and fifths.

Major triads are built with the *major* third and the *perfect* fifth.

Minor triads are built with the *minor* third and the *perfect* fifth.

Diminished triads are built with the *minor* third and the *diminished* fifth.

Augmented triads are built with the *major* third and the *augmented* fifth.

Figure 13.12

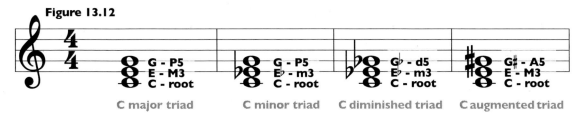

If you feel that you need a bit more review of the triad qualities, read chapter 9 and review the exercises.

Roman Numerals

We can combine the concepts of triad qualities and scales to create diatonic triads. Diatonic triads are triads that use only the notes of a given key or scale. If we take the notes of a G major scale and build a triad on each note, we get diatonic triads.

Using our knowledge of intervals, we can assess the quality of each triad. We find that the qualities of the chords form a pattern: major, minor, minor, major, major, minor, diminished. These qualities will be the same for all diatonic triads in all major keys.

We can use Roman numerals to discuss these qualities as well. Roman numerals are helpful because they can communicate a number of different ideas about the notes in a piece of music:

Roman numerals communicate

1. the scale degree number,

2. the scale degree name, and

3. the quality of the chord.

Roman numerals can also be easily adjusted to communicate notes or chords outside the key.

Figure 13.13 Diatonic triads of a major scale

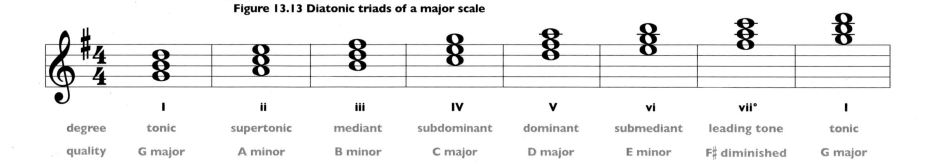

degree	I	ii	iii	IV	V	vi	vii°	I
quality	G major	A minor	B minor	C major	D major	E minor	F♯ diminished	G major

degree names: tonic, supertonic, mediant, subdominant, dominant, submediant, leading tone, tonic

You will notice in Figure 13.13 that there are capital and lowercase Roman numerals.

Capital Roman numerals refer to the major triads, while lowercase symbols refer to the minor triads. The diminished triads are lowercase Roman numerals with a ∘ sign. When augmented triads are used, the Roman numerals are capital and include a + sign.

The number given to a triad is based upon how that triad relates to the given key.

If you feel that you need a bit more review of the diatonic triads and Roman numerals, read chapter 10 and review the exercises.

Triad Inversions with Roman Numerals

An **inverted triad** occurs when the notes are rearranged so that the root is no longer the lowest sounding pitch. A triad is built on three notes, the root–third–fifth.

A root position triad is one where the root of the triad is the lowest-sounding pitch. A first inversion triad is one where the third is the lowest-sounding pitch. A second inversion triad is one where the fifth is the lowest-sounding pitch.

Figure 13.14

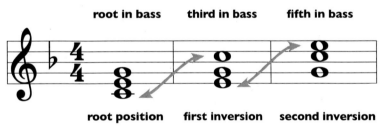

We can express these inversions within the context of Roman numerals by adding numbers next to them.

Figure 13.15

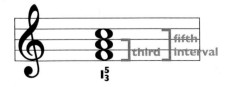

BONUS

When transposing a piece after doing Roman numeral analysis, follow the steps for transposing from chapter 7. Remember that Roman numeral analysis communicates the scale degree number.

In the case of a first inversion triad, we add the number 6 to the right of the Roman numeral.

Figure 13.16

In the case of a second inversion triad, we add the number 6 and 4 to the right of the Roman numeral.

Figure 13.17

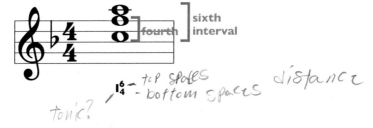

If you feel that you need a bit more review of triad inversions, or if you would like to review putting them into practice when analyzing music, read chapters 11 and 12. You may also want to review the exercises from those chapters as well.

What Have I Learned?
and where do we go from here?

I hope that *Math in Motion* has given you a foundation for how to analyze a musical score. This tool gives you the ability to discover the chord progressions composers employ. Score analysis gives you creative insights into any style or genre of music. All of the music you considered too intimidating to learn will now be accessible. A proper analysis creates bridges for learning a new song or composing a new piece.

Even if you do not play an instrument, the techniques you have learned in this book have prepared you to begin. The best place to begin is with your instrument's notes: where are the specific notes? How do you produce an E, an F, or a D♯? Once you understand the keyboard, the relationships between notes, chords, and key signatures can all be developed for discovery and creativity.

Another important step in cultivating your musical ability is simply to listen to music. One of the best American composers, Aaron Copland, said, "If you want to understand music better, you can do nothing more important than listen to it." Beyond this, I would encourage you to listen to music outside of your usual preferences. We tend to neglect listening to music that is not in accord with our tastes. So much of the time we live as though music belongs to us as individuals. I would encourage you to challenge your ear and listen to all sorts of music from all possible time periods. In addition, be sure to listen to music with others. Do not isolate your musical habits to time spent alone. Share your music discoveries with your friends, family, and teachers. Be willing to allow others to challenge your tastes, and humbly challenge others in their tastes.

Without craftsmanship, inspiration is a mere reed shaken in the wind.

—Johannes Brahms

Nurturing good habits of listening to music will gradually give you an arsenal for melodies and variations of melodies to use within chord progressions. The more you listen to music with purpose, the more you train your ear to understand the elements of music so that you can be creative. God created us with a desire for creativity because He uses humanity as instruments to fill the entire earth with His glory. This is our mission on earth. We participate in studies like music theory to discover expressions of God's beauty in this world and to fill the earth with this beauty.

I listened more than I studied...thus, little by little my knowledge and ability were developed.

—Franz Joseph Haydn

Supplemental Material

Harmonic and Melodic Minor Scales

Read this section after chapter 7.

In chapter 5 we learned about natural minor scales. The natural minor scale is a series of eight notes containing this specific pattern of whole steps and half steps in ascending order: W–H–W–W–H–W–W.

Figure S.1 E Natural minor

An important feature of the natural minor scale is the whole step between the $\hat{7}$ (subtonic) to the upper $\hat{1}$ (tonic). Throughout history, musicians and composers experimented with this whole step. Many raised the seventh scale degree to create a half step (leading tone) from the seventh scale degree to the tonic. The raised note eventually gave way to two additional forms of the minor scale: harmonic minor and melodic minor.

The **harmonic minor scale** is based on the natural minor scale but raises the seventh scale degree by a half step. For example, take the E natural minor scale (see Figure S.1 above).

To create the harmonic form of the minor scale you take the existing natural minor scale and raise the seventh scale degree by one half step. In the case of E minor, we raise the D up by half step to D♯ (see Figure S.2, next page). The notes in E harmonic minor are therefore: E–F♯–G–A–B–C–D♯–E. Try to find a way to listen to this scale. Do you hear the pull to the tonic?

Figure S.2 E Harmonic minor scale

Like the harmonic minor scale, the **melodic minor scale** uses the existing natural minor scale and raises both the sixth and seventh scale degrees by a half step. This means that we would take the existing E natural minor scale and raise the sixth and seventh scale degrees from C and D to C♯ and D♯, respectively.

Figure S.3 E Melodic minor scale

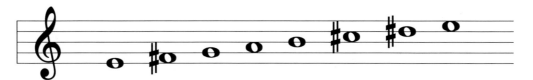

It is important to understand that in the harmonic and melodic minor scales, notes will always be raised by one half step from their natural minor position. To see this, let's create an F melodic minor scale. To begin, use the pattern of half steps and whole steps for a natural minor scale. The F natural minor scale contains the notes F–G–A♭–B♭–C–D♭–E♭–F.

Figure S.4 F Natural minor scale

To create the F melodic minor scale, we simply raise the sixth and seventh scale degrees, D♭ and E♭, up by one half step. This changes the notes D♭ and E♭ to the notes D and E.

Figure S.5 F Melodic minor scale

Activity S.1

Write out the minor scales indicated. Remember, you should always begin with the natural form of the minor scale and make adjustments (such as a raised seventh degree scale) as needed.

A harmonic minor

B natural minor

G melodic minor

C harmonic minor

When working with different forms of the minor scale, it is important to realize that the minor scales do not change the key signature. Rather, the harmonic and melodic minor scales are expressed with accidentals outside the given key signature.

The melody below is in the key of D minor. Notice how the seventh scale degree, the C, has been raised by half step to C♯.

Figure S.6

Since this piece has a raised seventh scale degree, it is using the D harmonic minor scale. Observe how the key signature is not changed to include the C♯, but rather that the C♯ is added into the music when it is supposed to be played. When using the harmonic or melodic minor scales, it is customary to use the key signature for the natural minor scale and add the raised notes into the music.

Harmonic and Melodic Minor and Harmony

Read this section after chapter 10.

In chapter 10, you learned about diatonic triad qualities in both major and minor keys. The triad qualities for the natural minor scales were: minor, diminished, major, minor, minor, major, and major as the figure below illustrates.

Figure S.7 E Natural minor triads

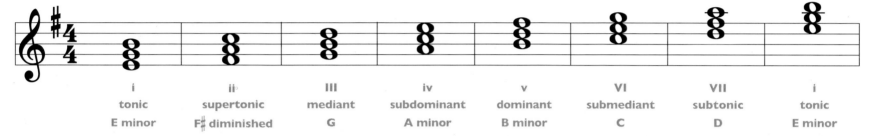

i	ii°	III	iv	v	VI	VII	i
tonic	supertonic	mediant	subdominant	dominant	submediant	subtonic	tonic
E minor	F♯ diminished	G	A minor	B minor	C	D	E minor

In the discussion above this one, you learned about different forms of minor scales and how these new forms of minor adjust the natural minor scale by raising notes. These changes to the notes in the natural minor scale also change the harmony, as the harmony is based upon the notes in the given scale. When we make changes to the scale we also make changes to the harmony. Therefore, triad qualities for both the harmonic and melodic minor scales will differ from their natural minor counterpart.

Triads in Harmonic Minor

To illustrate how the adjusted notes change the harmony, let's look at the E harmonic minor. If you recall, the harmonic minor scale is built upon a natural minor scale. To create the harmonic minor scale, we take the natural minor scale and raise the seventh scale degree; thus, E harmonic minor contains the notes E–F♯–G–A–B–C–D♯–E. Now that we have added the D♯, we need to change all of the D notes to D♯.

Figure S.8 E Harmonic minor triads

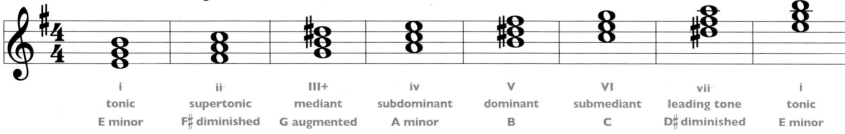

i	ii°	III+	iv	V	VI	vii°	i
tonic	supertonic	mediant	subdominant	dominant	submediant	leading tone	tonic
E minor	F♯ diminished	G augmented	A minor	B	C	D♯ diminished	E minor

In the Figure S.8, the D notes within the triads have been replaced with a D♯. This changes the quality of the third, fifth, and seventh chords. Using the techniques discussed in chapter 9, we can assess the intervals and thus the quality of those triads. We discover that the quality of the three chord is augmented as it contains a major third and augmented fifth above the root, the quality of the five chord is major as it contains a major third and perfect fifth above the root, and the quality of the seven chord is diminished as it contains a minor third and diminished fifth above the root. These triad qualities will be the same for all types of harmonic minor scales.

Triads in Melodic Minor

E melodic minor contains the notes E–F♯–G–A–B–C♯–D♯–E. To create this scale, start with the E natural minor scale (see Figure S.7) and raise the sixth and seventh scale degrees by a half step. These new notes have been added to the diatonic triads in the figure below and have thus changed the qualities.

Figure S.9 E Melodic minor triads

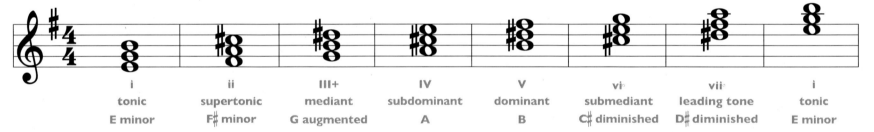

The new notes C♯ and D♯ change all triads except the first and last ones. The triad qualities for the melodic minor scale are, as seen above, minor, minor, augmented, major, major, diminished, and diminished. This pattern of triads is the same for all melodic minor scales.

Seventh Chords

Read this section after chapter 12.

In chapters 9, 10, 11, and 12 we learned how to interact with triads on various levels. Recall that we defined triads as simple chords that are formed with three notes: root, third, and fifth. In this section we will build upon your understanding of triads to create what is known as a **seventh chord**. A seventh chord is a more complex chord that contains four different notes: root, third, fifth, and seventh. An easy way to understand seventh chords is to realize that they are triads with an additional note, the seventh.

Figure S.10

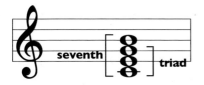

Like triads, seventh chords have different qualities. There are five different seventh chord qualities: major seventh, minor seventh, major-minor seventh, half-diminished seventh, and fully diminished seventh. These seventh chords are built on an existing triad quality with different types of seventh intervals above the root. Figure S.11 demonstrates each type of seventh chord. Notice how each type is a triad with some sort of seventh above the root.

BONUS

The major-minor seventh chord is often called the dominant seventh.

Figure S.11

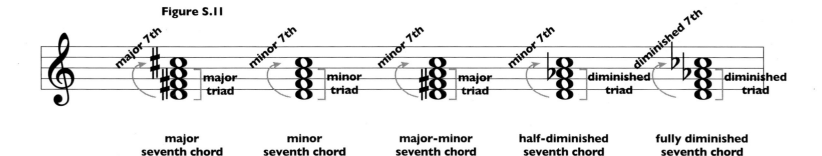

| major seventh chord | minor seventh chord | major-minor seventh chord | half-diminished seventh chord | fully diminished seventh chord |

Seventh Chords

major seventh chord	minor seventh chord	major-minor seventh chord	half-diminished seventh chord	fully diminished seventh chord
major triad (R-M3-P5)	minor triad (R-m3-P5)	major triad (R-M3-P5)	diminished triad (R-m3-d5)	diminished triad (R-m3-d5)
+	+	+	+	+
major seventh (M7) interval above the root	minor seventh (m7) interval above the root	minor seventh (m7) interval above the root	minor seventh (m7) interval above the root	diminished seventh (d7) interval above the root

To be able to work with seventh chords easily, you must have a strong understanding of basic triad types. If you can identify triad types successfully, you simply need to assess one more note and can identify the type of seventh chord.

 # Helpful Tools

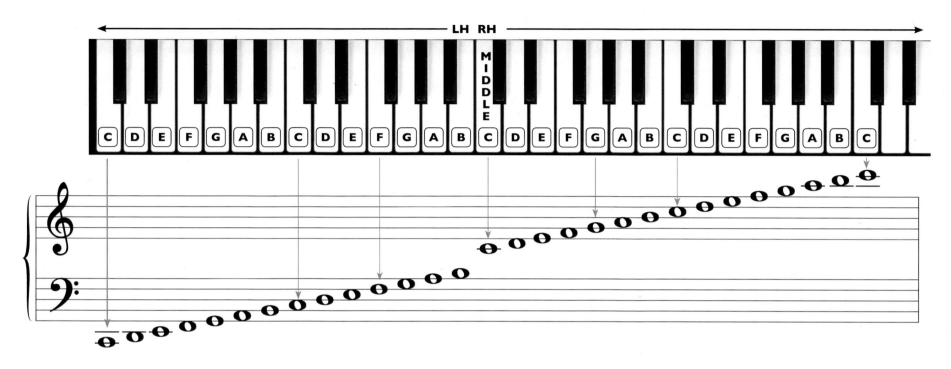

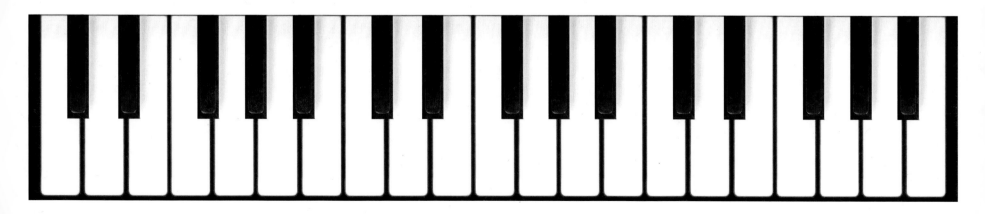

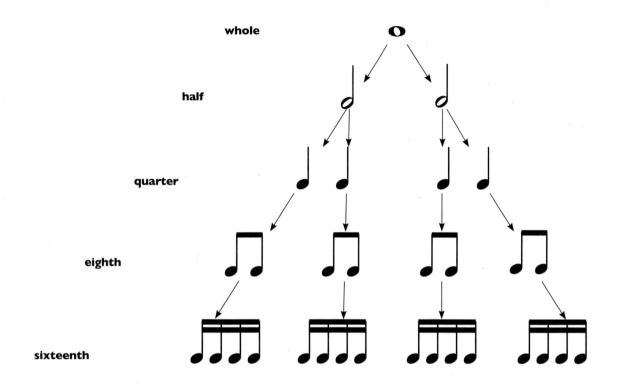

whole

half

quarter

eighth

sixteenth

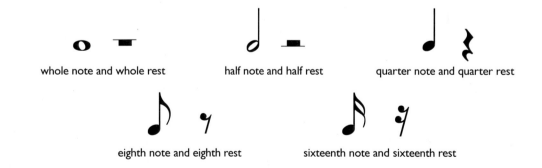

whole note and whole rest   half note and half rest   quarter note and quarter rest

eighth note and eighth rest   sixteenth note and sixteenth rest

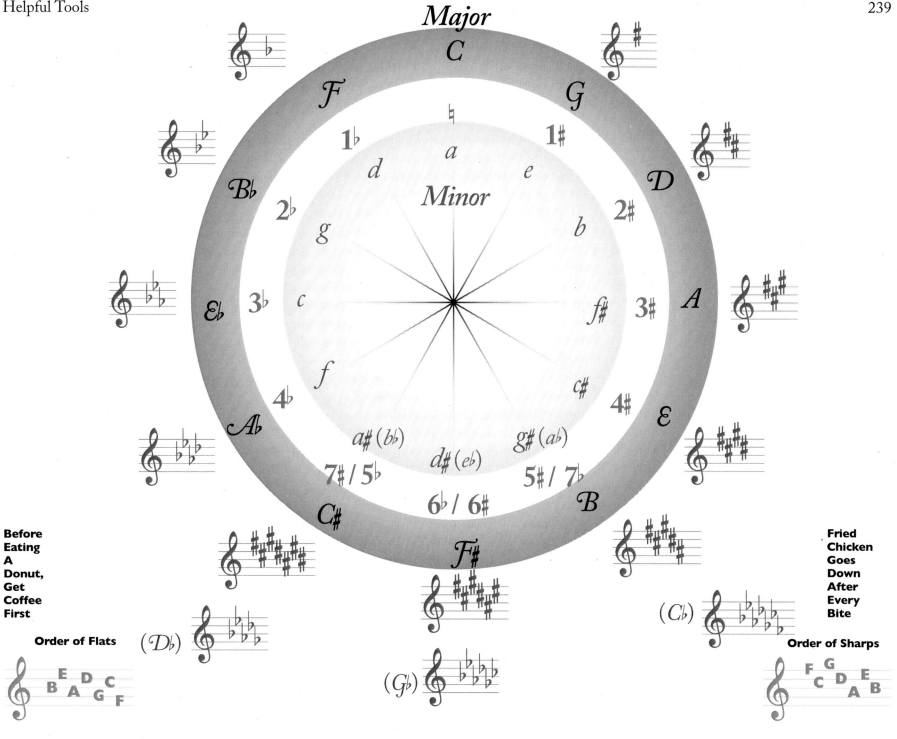

Before
Eating
A
Donut,
Get
Coffee
First

Order of Flats

Fried
Chicken
Goes
Down
After
Every
Bite

Order of Sharps

Score Analysis Project

"Kinda" big deal (handwritten)

This score analysis project may be used as a culminating activity to allow students to practice what they have learned through this book. Before students begin their projects, we recommend that they review the project help in the appendix.

we don't know yet (handwritten)

that's ok (handwritten)

The assignment is to complete a score analysis using Roman numerals (including inversions) on three different scores. There are six scores following these pages; we recommend that students choose two from those, and then choose the third from an outside resource (though students are welcome to choose three from the selections available). Please carefully read the requirements below to correctly execute the project.

Each score analysis should include:

- The key signature and the relative minor;
- The time signature from the top of the piece, along with an explanation of what the specific time signature means;
- A score analysis using Roman numerals (including inversions) (chapters 10–13).

Students also should:

- Label at least six different intervals throughout each score;
- Transpose one score to another key (you may copy and use the blank staves in the Helpful Tools section of this book).

At the end of the term of study, students may be asked to present their score analyses to a group. This time of presentation allows students to demonstrate their understanding of the music theory concepts presented in this book. Students may also be invited to perform a piece on an instrument either as a solo or as an ensemble with other students, or play a recording of a chosen piece of music. Use your imagination to involve the entire group in this celebration of music!

Sample Project Score

Key signature: B♭ major

Time signature: $\frac{4}{4}$: 4 beats per measure with the quarter note getting the beat.

Relative key signature: G minor

Intervals labeled below with boxes

Score analysis below

 # Anthology of Scores

"Be Thou My Vision"

Tune name	"Slane"
Text	Attributed to Irish poet, Saint Dallan Forgaill, c. 6th century
Translated by Mary E. Byrne, 1905	
Versified by Eleanor H. Hull, 1912	
Music	Irish melody
Meter	10 10.10 10

Where there is no vision the people perish: but he that keepeth the law, happy is he.

Proverbs 29:18

The tune "Slane" is named after a hill near Tara, Ireland, where Saint Patrick is believed to have challenged King Lóegaire by lighting the Paschal fire on the night before Easter Sunday as part of the Easter Vigil. This fire broke a law forbidding fires. The tune has been harmonized by many musicians, but it is generally agreed that the tune should be sung in unison. Saint Dollan Forgaill was an Irish Christian poet and writer around the end of the sixth century. He was known for his eulogies for Irish saints. According to some sources, he studied so intensely that he lost his sight, earning him the nickname "Dallan," meaning "little blind one."

sung at funerals

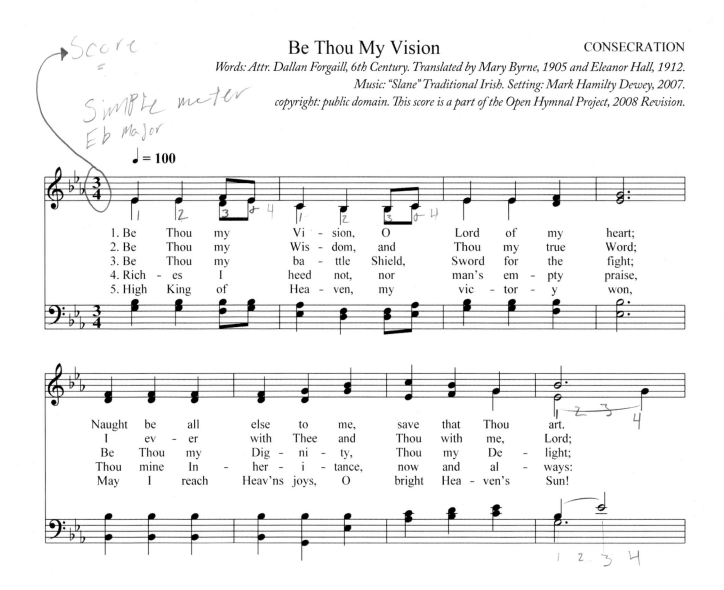

Score =
SIMPLE meter
Eb Major

Be Thou My Vision

CONSECRATION

Words: Attr. Dallan Forgaill, 6th Century. Translated by Mary Byrne, 1905 and Eleanor Hall, 1912.
Music: "Slane" Traditional Irish. Setting: Mark Hamilty Dewey, 2007.
copyright: public domain. This score is a part of the Open Hymnal Project, 2008 Revision.

Jn 16:13. Num 12:6

10 10 10 10

"Jesu, Joy of Man's Desiring"

Tune name   "Jesus bleibet meine Freude" (10th movement from "Herz und Mund und Tat und Leben" (Heart and Mouth and Deed and Life), BWV 147

Text   none

Music   Johannes Sebastian Bach

Arrangement for piano   Myra Hess, 1926

Simplified arrangement for piano (Measures 1–9)—Classical Conversations®, Inc.

"Herz und Mund und Tat und Leben" was a cantata for solo voices, chorus, and orchestra written by Johannes Sebastian Bach for the fourth Sunday of Advent. The tenth movement called "Jesus bleibet meine freude" (Jesu, Joy of Man's Desiring) is one of Bach's most cherished works. Today, this piece is often played at weddings during the bridal ceremony. Dame Myra Hess arranged the piano edition for this piece in 1926. Today, "Jesu, Joy of Man's Desiring" is one of the most respected pieces in music history.

Jesu, Joy of Man's Desiring

Johann Sebastian Bach
Classical Conversations®, Inc. Edition

"Old Hundredth (Doxology)"

Tune name	"Old Hundredth"
Text	Thomas Ken and Isaac Watts
Music	Louis Bourgeois
Meter	88.88

Make a joyful noise unto the LORD, all ye lands. Serve the LORD with gladness: come before his presence with singing. Know ye that the LORD he is God: it is he that hath made us, and not we ourselves; we are his people and the sheep of his pasture.

Psalm 100:1–3

The first verse of this well-known hymn became known as the "Doxology" and is said to be the most commonly sung of any song in the last three centuries. Some believe this verse has done more for the doctrine of the Trinity than any other text or book. The author of the text, Bishop Thomas Ken (1637–1711), wrote a number of hymns but was better known as one of the first hymn writers to write words outside versifications of Psalms and canticles taken from Scripture. The tune "Old Hundredth" is one of the most famous tunes in all of Christian hymnody, written by Louis Bourgeois. Louis Bourgeois was a devoted follower of John Calvin and moved to Geneva, Switzerland, to join the Reformation movement during the middle of the sixteenth century. It was in Geneva that Bourgeois collaborated with Calvin on writing the Psalms to accessible meter, known as the Genevan Psalter (1562). The tune later appeared in William Kethe's version of Psalm 100, "All People That on Earth Do Dwell." This tune became known in England as "The Hundredth" but was later given the title "Old Hundredth" in future hymnal publications to show the tune was originally from the "Old" Psalter in Geneva.

Old Hundredth

(From All That Dwells Below the Skies)

This famous tune in the style of a German choral first appeared in the Geneva Psalter about 1555. The four lines of the Doxology were written by Bishop Thomas Ken (1637–1711). The other set of words given here were written by Isaac Watts (1674–1748), one of the greatest of English hymn writers.

Thos. Ken
Isaac Watts

Louis Bourgeois (?)

Praise God, from whom all bless-ings flow; Praise Him, all crea-tures here be - low; Praise

Him a - bove, ye heav'n - ly host; Praise Fa - ther, Son, and Ho - ly Ghost.

Copyright, 1917, by
C. C. BIRCHARD & COMPANY

Source: Dykema, Peter, Will Earhart, Osbourne McConathy, and Hollis Dann. *I Hear America Singing: 55 Songs and Choruses for Community Singing.* Boston,: C. C. Birchard & Company, 1917.

"There Is a Fountain"

Tune name	"Cleansing Fountain"
Text	William Cowper
Music	American melody
Meter	86.86.66.86

In that day there shall be a fountain opened to the house of David and to the inhabitants of Jerusalem for sin and for uncleanness.

Zechariah 13:1

William Cowper is considered one of the finest English writers of all time and was good friends with John Newton. Cowper and Newton combined to produce one of the most famous hymnals, the *Olney Hymns*, in 1799. "There Is a Fountain" is one of Cowper's most treasured hymns from this hymnal and was later put to an American folk tune that would have been commonly sung during the American camp revivals in the early nineteenth century. This tune would go on to become the staple for Cowper's text and is still sung today in churches throughout America.

There Is a Fountain

ZECHARIAH 13:1
William Cowper, *pub.* 1772

CLEANSING FOUNTAIN
attr. to Lowell Mason

Refrain

Lose	all	their	guilt	-	y	stains,	Lose	all	their	guilt	-	y	stains;
Washed	all	my	sins	a	-	way,	Washed	all	my	sins	a	-	way;
Are	safe,	to	sin	no		more,	Are	safe,	to	sin	no		more;
And	shall	be	till	I		die,	And	shall	be	till	I		die;
I'll	sing	Thy	pow'r	to		save,	I'll	sing	Thy	pow'r	to		save;

And	sin	-	ners	plunged	be	-	neath	the	flood	Lose	all	their	guilt	-	y	stains.
And	there	have	I,	though	vile		as	he,		Washed	all	my	sins	a	-	way.
Till	all	the	ran	-	somed	church	of	God		Are	safe,	to	sin	no		more.
Re	-	deem	-	ing	love	has	been	my	theme,	And	shall	be	till	I		die.
Then	in	a	no	-	bler,	sweet	-	er	song,	I'll	sing	Thy	pow'r	to		save.

"When I Survey the Wondrous Cross"

Tune name	"Hamburg"
Text	Isaac Watts, 1707
Music	From a Gregorian chant
Meter	88.88

But God forbid that I should glory, save in the cross of our Lord Jesus Christ, by whom the world is crucified unto me, and I unto the world.

Galatians 6:14

This hymn by Isaac Watts is sometimes labeled as the greatest hymn in the English language. Isaac Watts complained about the poor quality of worship music in his day until his father, tired of hearing his complaints, challenged the young Isaac to do something about it. Isaac Watts went on to write more than six hundred hymns and tunes for corporate worship and is known today as the "Father of English Hymnody." The famous American church musician Lowell Mason arranged the tune for Watts' hymn. Mason affirmed that he had arranged this tune from an old Gregorian chant, the oldest church music known today. The melody in this hymn contains only a five-note range, a consistent range to most chants in the early church.

When I Survey the Wondrous Cross

LENT

Words: Isaac Watts, 1707.
Music: 'Hamburg', Lowell Mason, 1824. Setting: "Northfield Hymnal", 1904.
copyright: public domain. This score is a part of the Open Hymnal Project, 2014 Revision.

1. When I sur - vey the won - drous cross
2. For - bid it, Lord, that I should boast,
3. See from His head, His hands, His feet,
4. His dy - ing crim - son, like a robe,
5. Were the whole realm of na - ture mine,

On which the Prince of Glo - ry died,
Save in the death of Christ my God!
Sor - row and love flow min - gled down!
Spreads o'er His bo - dy on the tree;
That were a pre - sent far too small;

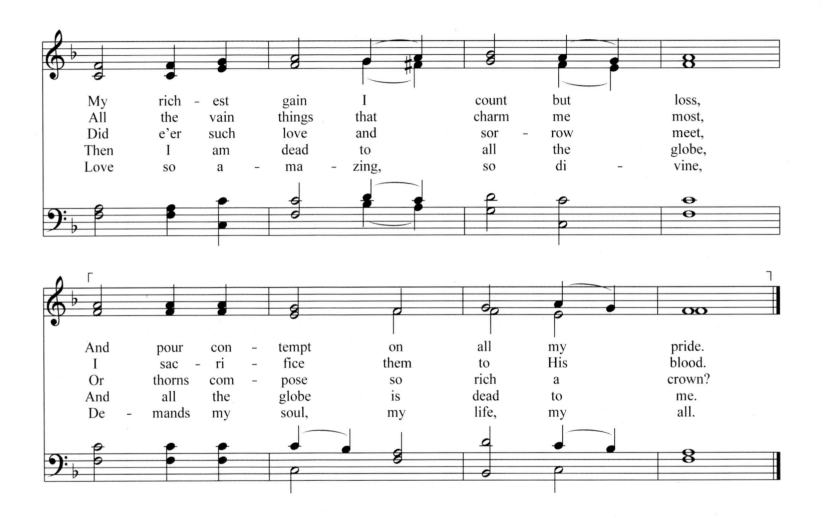

My   rich - est   gain   I   count   but   loss,
All   the   vain   things   that   charm   me   most,
Did   e'er   such   love   and   sor - row   meet,
Then   I   am   dead   to   all   the   globe,
Love   so   a - ma - zing,   so   di - vine,

And   pour   con - tempt   on   all   my   pride.
I   sac - ri - fice   them   to   His   blood.
Or   thorns   com - pose   so   rich   a   crown?
And   all   the   globe   is   dead   to   me.
De - mands   my   soul,   my   life,   my   all.

Gal 6:14, Rom 7:24   *8 8 8 8*

"When Peace Like a River"

Tune name	"Ville du Havre"
Text	Horatio G. Spafford
Music	Philip P. Bliss
Meter	11 8 11 9 with Chorus

God is our refuge and strength, a very present help in trouble.

Psalm 46:1

This hymn was written by a Presbyterian from Chicago named Horatio Spafford. Spafford was a wealthy lawyer and a well-known businessman in the Chicago area. The Chicago Fire in 1871 wiped out most of his business, and he turned his attention toward his good friend D. L. Moody and his work in Great Britain. In 1873, Spafford had arranged a family trip for his wife and four daughters to visit Moody. Spafford stayed behind in Chicago to take care of some business and planned to meet up with his family in Britain a few days later. On November 22, the ship carrying his family struck another vessel and sank in under fifteen minutes. His four daughters drowned in the shipwreck, but his wife survived. When she arrived in England, she telegrammed her husband with the words "Survived alone." Spafford left immediately to go tend to his grieving wife, and it is believed that he penned the words to this wonderful hymn when passing through the area where his four daughters had drowned. Gospel hymn writer Philip Bliss was so impressed with Spafford's faith during his tragic loss that he wrote music for Spafford's words. Bliss later named the tune "Ville du Havre" after the name of the shipwrecked vessel.

When Peace Like a River

taught me to say, "It is well, it is well with my soul."
help - less es - tate, and has shed his own blood for my soul.
bear it no more; praise the Lord, praise the Lord, O my soul!

Text: Horatio G. Spafford, 1873
Tune: Philip P. Bliss, 1876

11 8 11 9 with refrain
VILLE DU HAVRE
www.hymnary.org/text/when_peace_like_a_river_attendeth_my_way

Refrain (may be sung after final stanza only)

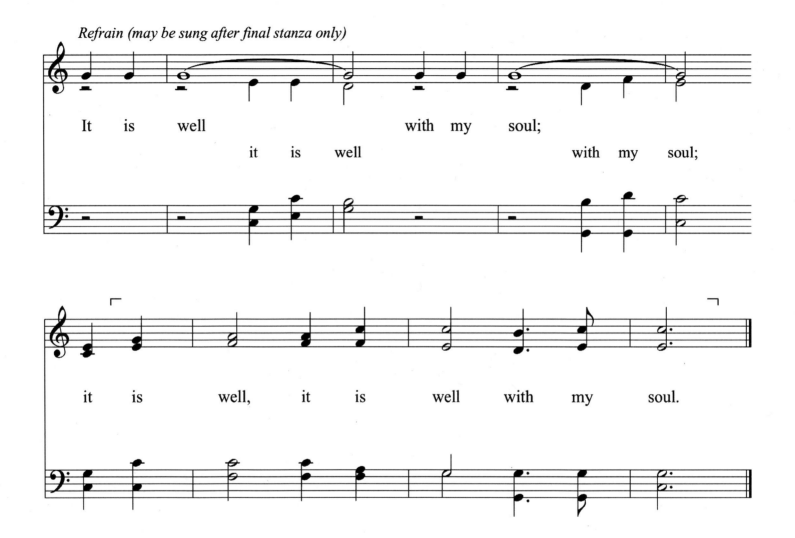

It   is   well   with   my   soul;
      it   is   well   with   my   soul;

it   is   well,   it   is   well   with   my   soul.

For Further Reading

Apel, Willi. *Harvard Dictionary of Music*. 2nd ed., Belknap Press of Harvard University Press, 1969.

Clendinning, Jane Piper, and Elizabeth West Marvin. *The Musician's Guide to Theory and Analysis*. 2nd ed., Norton, 2011.

Kinchen, John D., and Gabriel Miller. *Music Theory for the Christian Musician*. Academx Publishing Services, Inc., 2015.

Kostka, Stefan M., and Dorothy Payne. *Tonal Harmony: With an Introduction to Twentieth-Century Music*. 6th ed., McGraw-Hill, 2009.

Laitz, Steven G. *The Complete Musician: An Integrated Approach to Tonal Theory, Analysis, and Listening*. 3rd ed., Oxford University Press, 2012.

Osbeck, Kenneth W. *101 Hymn Stories: The Inspiring True Stories Behind 101 Favorite Hymns*. Grand Rapids: Kregel Publications, 2012.

---. *101 More Hymn Stories: The Inspiring True Stories Behind 101 Favorite Hymns*. Grand Rapids: Kregel Publications, 2013.

Roig-Francolí, Miguel A. *Harmony in Context*. second ed., McGraw-Hill, 2011.

Project Help

This section will help prepare you for your final project. Each song title has been listed along with some general considerations. You will also find an explanation of more complex chords found in the scores. There are a few chords within the scores used in this book that were not taught in this curriculum. The brief explanation of the concepts behind them should help answer any questions.

"Be Thou my Vision"
General Considerations and Approach

As you work through your Roman numeral analysis of this piece, keep in mind that duplicate notes are common. Many hymns, this one in particular, have duplicate notes. Recall that you should only count these notes once. In addition, there are a few instances where you will need to consider implied notes, meaning that not all notes of the triad will be present. For this, remember that the root must be present in order to call a chord by that name.

"Jesu, Joy of Man's Desiring"
General Considerations and Approach

This piece is more difficult than others in the text due to the nature of the notes in the treble clef. The other scores in the text feature vertical stacks of notes with mostly the same value. This piece has a note equal in value to one beat in the left hand with a melodic line over top of it in the treble clef. While this piece is more challenging, analysis is possible; it will require a unique approach.

When analyzing this piece, use the following rules.

Rule one: Assume that the given note in the bass clef is the root of the triad.

Rule two: Confirm the assumption by assessing the notes in the treble clef. Look for duplicate notes of the bass and for other notes in the assumed triad.

Let's look at Figure A.1, which is taken from the first beat of measure one, to see these steps in action. The note in the bass clef is a D. Using our first rule for this piece, we assume that D is the root of the triad and that said triad is D or I $\frac{5}{3}$ in the key.

Figure A.1

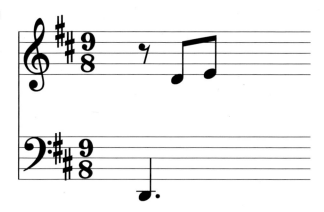

To confirm this assumption, we look at the notes in the treble clef. We will consider both the D and E as they are both played during the bass note D. As there are two Ds in this section, our original assumption, I $\frac{5}{3}$, seems like the best option. The notes F♯ and A are implied and not present. The E, however, is not part of the triad and should be ignored.

It is important to see that the bass note will not always serve as the root of the triad. To see this, let's look at an additional example. Figure A.2 is taken from part of the third beat of measure three.

Figure A.2

Rule one states we are to assume that the given bass note serves as the root for the triad. Since the bass note is G, we will assume that it is a G triad or IV $_3^5$ in the key. The second rule states that we should look at the notes in the treble clef to confirm the assumption. The notes in the treble clef are E and F♯. If the triad is G, as assumed, we would expect to see a B or a D; however, we see an E and F♯. From this, we can see that the assumption that G is the root was not confirmed by the notes in the treble clef and rather that the triad E minor is more likely: E (root) and G (third).

While analysis of this piece can be more challenging, it is well within your grasp and ability.

Complex Chord Explanations

Figure A.3 "Jesu, Joy of Man's Desiring"

The excerpt in Figure A.3 is measure four of "Jesu, Joy of Man's Desiring." The chord labeled here contains the notes A, G, F♯ and E. Rule one states that we should assume that the bass note A is the root of triad. If we look at notes in the treble clef, we can see that assumption confirmed by the note E. In addition, the G is a seventh interval up from the A note, communicating a partial A major seventh chord. (For more information on seventh chords, see Supplemental Material.) **You can analyze this chord by labeling it as an A major triad root position**.

Figure A.4 "Jesu, Joy of Man's Desiring"

The excerpt in Figure A.4 is measure seven of "Jesu, Joy of Man's Desiring." The chord labeled here contains the notes, G♯, F♯, E, and D. Using rules one and two we could see this chord as either a G♯ diminished or an E major in first inversion. In either reading, this chord is part of a larger group of chromatic (meaning outside the key signature) chords called secondary chords. This chord is altered outside the key to tonicize (place more emphasis on) the next chord. While this chord goes beyond this text, you can find several explanations on the Internet by searching "secondary dominants" or "secondary diminished chords." **For now, think of this chord as an E major in first inversion or a G♯ diminished in root position. The actual Roman numeral depending on your answer: V $_5^6$/V (E major in first inversion) or vii°⁷/V (G♯ diminished) respectively.**

"Old Hundredth"
General Considerations and Approach

As you work through your Roman numeral analysis of this piece, keep in mind that extra notes are common and that these extra notes should be ignored. A few of these extra notes create seventh chords, a chord beyond a triad; if you want to learn about seventh chords, go to the Supplemental Material section. In addition, there are a few instances where you will need to consider implied notes, meaning that not all notes of the triad will be present. For this, remember that the root must be present in order to call a chord by that name.

"There is a Fountain"
General Considerations and Approach

Remember that duplicate notes will occur throughout this piece and that you should only count these notes once. Also, you may find extra notes in a few places, particularly when eighth notes are present. In these instances, you should work to find a triad and simply ignore any notes that do not fit within that triad. In this piece, you may also find places where the notes in the bass clef remain the same while the notes in the treble clef change. For this, you should see if any triads are created by the change of notes. If you find an additional triad, label it; however, if you do not find an additional triad, you can ignore these extra notes as they are not part of the triad. A few of these extra notes create seventh chords, a chord beyond a triad. If you want to learn about seventh chords, go to the Supplemental Material section.

"When I Survey the Wondrous Cross"
General Considerations and Approach

As you work through this score, be sure to count duplicate notes only once. You will encounter extra notes in several of the chords. Remember that you should always attempt to find an order of notes in which all of the pitches are on lines and/or spaces. Once you find a triad, you can ignore any remaining notes not in the triad. Many of the chords with extra notes in this score are called seventh chords. If you wish to learn about this more complex chord structure, please read the Supplemental Material section.

Figure A.5 "When I Survey the Wondrous Cross"

Complex Chord Explanations

The excerpt in Figure A.5 is measure two of "When I Survey the Wondrous Cross." The labeled section occurs again on measure ten. The notes in the triad are F♯, A, A, and C. If we count the duplicate note once, F♯, A, and C remain. Using intervals, we see that we have a root-m3-d5 and thus a diminished triad. The challenge with this is that the chord is outside the key and goes beyond what is discussed in the text. This F♯ diminished triad is a type of secondary chord. The altered quality of diminished emphasizes the chord that follows by creating a vii° to I movement. **Label the chord as an F♯ diminished triad in first inversion. In more advanced theory, we would label it as a vii°⁶/ii (seven diminished six of two).**

Figure A.6 "When I Survey the Wondrous Cross"

The excerpt in Figure A.6 is measure three of "When I Survey the Wondrous Cross." This same chord movement also occurs on measure eleven of this piece. The half notes in the bass clef have the same duration as the pairs of quarter notes in the treble clef. When this occurs, it is best to see if different triads are formed or if some of the notes are extra notes and should be ignored. The notes in the bass clef and first set of quarter notes are C, F, and A. This is an F major triad in second inversion. Now that we have successfully identified a triad, you should look to see if the other notes form a different triad or if they are extra notes. The second group of quarter notes, E and G, with the bass clef notes, both C, create a C major triad in root position. As two different triads are created, we should label them as such. **The first grouping of quarter notes is an F major triad in second inversion and the second grouping is a C major triad in root position.**

Figure A.7 "When I Survey the Wondrous Cross"

The excerpt in Figure A.7 is measure fifteen of "When I Survey the Wondrous Cross." The chord labeled here contains the notes B♭, D, F, and G. You should be able to recognize a couple of possible triads in this collection of notes. The notes G, B♭, and D make up a G minor triad while the notes B♭, D, and F make up a B♭ major triad. Since both of these readings cannot be correct, you should attempt to find an order of notes in which all four pitches are on lines or spaces. In doing so you will form a chord of four notes: the root, the third, the fifth, and the seventh.

We find that the notes G, B♭, D, and F create a G minor triad with an extra note F. The F in the chord is a seventh interval up from the G note, making the G minor triad a seventh chord. To learn more about seventh chords, read the Supplemental Material section. **You can answer this chord by labeling it a G minor triad in first inversion.**

Figure A.8 "When I Survey the Wondrous Cross"

The excerpt in Figure A.8 is measure fifteen of "When I Survey the Wondrous Cross." The half notes in the treble and bass clefs have the same duration as the quarter notes in those clefs. When this occurs, it is best to see if the different notes form different triads or if some of the notes are extra notes and should be ignored. The half notes and first set of quarter notes give us the notes C, E, and A. This is an A minor triad in first inversion. Now that we have successfully identified a triad, you should look to see if the other notes form a different triad or if they are extra notes. When combined with the existing notes C and E, the B♭ and G create a C major-minor seventh chord in root position. To learn more about seventh chords, please read the Supplemental Material section. As two different chord are created, you should label them as such. **The first grouping of quarter notes is an A minor triad in first inversion, and the second grouping is a C major triad in root position.**

"When Peace Like A River"

General Considerations and Approach

As you work through this score, be sure to count duplicate notes only once. You will encounter extra notes in several of the chords. Remember that you should always attempt to find an order of notes in which all of the pitches are on lines and/or spaces. Once you find a triad, you can ignore any remaining notes not in the triad. Many of the chords with extra notes in this score are called seventh chords, explained in the Supplemental Material.

Complex Chord Explanations

Figure A.9 "When Peace Like a River"

The excerpt in Figure A.9 is measure one of "When Peace Like a River." The chord labeled here contains the notes C, G, D, and F. There are a few different possible triads between these notes. C and G both fit into a C major triad, D and F both fit into a D minor triad, and C and F both fit into an F major triad. The way to discern this triad name is to look at which note is on the very bottom of the bass clef. The note on the bottom is the C. This helps you in identifying the chord as a C chord. The notes D and F are called passing tones and go beyond the scope of this text. **You can answer this chord by labeling it a C major triad root position.**

Figure A.10 "When Peace Like a River"

The excerpt in Figure A.10 is measure two of "When Peace Like a River." The chord labeled here contains the notes F, G, B, and D. You should be able to recognize a couple of possible triads in this collection of notes. The notes G, B, and D make up a G major triad while the notes B, D, and F make up a B diminished triad. Since both of these readings cannot be correct, you should attempt to find an order of notes in which all four pitches are on lines or spaces. In doing so you will form a chord of four notes: the root, the third, the fifth, and the seventh. We find that the notes G, B, D, and F create a G major triad with an extra note F. The problem is that the F note is in the bass. The chord is called a G major-minor seventh chord in third inversion. **You can label this chord as G major root position.**

Figure A.11 "When Peace Like a River"

The excerpt in Figure A.11 is measure three of "When Peace Like a River." The chord labeled here contains the notes D, G, B, F, and A. You should include the two quarter notes in the analysis as they are both played while the half notes are sustained. You should be able to recognize that there are a few possible triads in this collection of notes. With the notes B, D, and F, there is a B diminished triad. With the notes G, B, and D, there is a G major triad. The notes D, F, and A create a D minor triad. Since all three of these readings cannot be correct, you should attempt to find an order of notes in which all of the pitches are on lines or spaces. By doing this, you will find that we have a G major triad with additional notes F and A. The F added to the G major triad makes the chord a G major-minor seventh chord. The A on the second beat is called an appoggiatura; it is a non-chord tone (a note that is not part of the chord) that creates a tension and release as it resolves down to the G in the third beat. **You can answer this chord by labeling it a G major triad second inversion.**

Figure A.12 "When Peace Like a River"

The excerpt in Figure A.12 is measure five of "When Peace Like a River." The chord labeled here contains the notes B, D, G♯, and B. The chord is a G♯ diminished triad with the B acting as the minor third and the D acting as the diminished fifth. The chord is outside the key and goes beyond what is discussed in the text. This G♯ diminished triad is a type of secondary chord. The altered quality of a diminished chord emphasizes the chord that follows by creating a vii° to I movement. **You can answer this chord by labeling it a G♯ diminished in first inversion. In more advanced theory, we would label it as a vii°⁶/vi.**

Figure A.13 "When Peace Like a River"

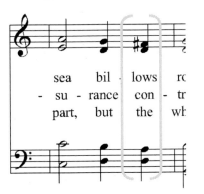

The excerpt in Figure A.13 is measure six of "When Peace Like a River." You will also see a chord similar to this one in measure 10. The chord here contains the notes D, A, and F♯. The chord is a D major triad with the F♯ acting as the major third and the A acting as the perfect fifth. The chord is outside the key and goes beyond what is discussed in the text. This D major triad is a type of secondary chord. The accidental makes this a secondary dominant chord, V/V ("five of five") that tonicizes (places more emphasis on) the V chord in beat 1 of the next measure and creates a sense of tension and release. **You can answer this chord by labeling it a D major in root position. In more advanced theory, we would label it as a V$^5_3$/V.**

Figure A.14 "When Peace Like a River"

The excerpt in Figure A.14 is measure eight of "When Peace Like a River." The chord labeled here contains the notes E, C, G, and B. You should be able to recognize that there are a couple of possible triads in this collection of notes. The C, E, and G notes make up the C major triad, while the E, G, and B notes make up the E minor triad. Since both of these readings cannot be correct, you should attempt to find an order of notes in which all four pitches are on lines or spaces. In so doing you will form a chord of four notes: the root, the third, the fifth, and the seventh. By doing this you will find that we have a C major triad with an additional note B. The B in this chord is the seventh interval up from C and is a part of the C triad, making the chord a C major seventh chord. **You can answer this chord by labeling it a C major triad first inversion.**

Figure A.15 "When Peace Like a River"

lot,   thou   hast

gard - ed   my

cross,   and   I

The excerpt in Figure A.15 is measure nine of "When Peace Like a River." The chord contains the notes E, C♯, G, and A. From your lessons you should be able to recognize that there are a couple of possible triads in this collection of notes. With the notes C♯, E, and G, there is a C♯ diminished triad. With the notes A, C♯, and E, there is an A major triad. Since both of these readings cannot be correct, you should attempt to find an order of notes in which all four pitches are on lines or spaces. By doing this, you will find that we have an A major triad with an additional note G. This chord is a seventh chord. To find out more about seventh chords, read the Supplemental Material section. In addition, this chord is outside the key and goes beyond what is discussed in the text. This A major triad is a type of secondary chord. The accidental makes this a secondary dominant chord, V^7 of ii ("five seven of two"), that tonicizes (places more emphasis on) the ii chord in beat 1 of the next measure and creates a sense of tension and release. **You can answer this chord by labeling it a A major triad in second inversion. In more advanced theory, we would label it as a V_3^4/ii, "five four-three of two."**

Figure A.16 "When Peace Like a River"

say,   "It   is

tate,   and   has

more;   praise   the

The excerpt in Figure A.16 is measure eleven of "When Peace Like a River." The chord labeled here contains the notes G, C, G, and A. You should know that there is not one complete triad among these four notes. You are dealing with implied notes. Our confusion lies with the two possibilities of G and C (C major, implied E) or C and A (A minor, implied E). In advanced theory, this chord is actually an extension of an A minor triad. The correct answer to this chord analysis is an A minor seventh chord with an implied E note. **You can answer this chord by labeling it an A minor triad first inversion.**

 In-Class Activity Answer Key

Chapter 1
Activity 1.1

a) Write in the name of the notes on the blank lines you see on the keyboard in Figure 1.6.

b) If all the responses you provided in Figure 1.6 were lowered one half step (flatted), what would the names of the notes be?

E♭, G♭, B♭, E♭, E or F♭, A♭, B or C♭, D♭

c) If all the responses you provided in Figure 1.6 were raised one half step (sharped), what would the names of the notes be?

F or E♯, G♯, C or B♯, F or E♯, F♯, A♯, C♯, D♯

d) Name the enharmonic equivalents of each of the black keys, labeled a–d, below.

a. *A♯, B♭;* b. *D♯, E♭;* c. *C♯, D♭;* d. *G♯, A♭*

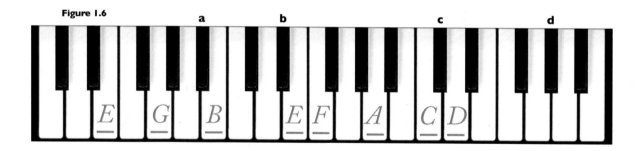

Figure 1.6

Chapter 2

Activity 2.1—In-class activity

Write four of each of the following note values on the staves below:

1) Whole notes
2) Half notes
3) Quarter notes
4) Eighth notes with a flag
5) Eighth note pairs beamed together
6) Sixteenth notes with two flags
7) Sixteenth note pairs beamed together

Responses will vary.

Chapter 3

Activity 3.1 — In-class activity

Identify the different types of meter (simple or compound) given the time signatures below:

$\frac{6}{8}$ *compound* $\frac{9}{16}$ *compound*

$\frac{4}{4}$ *simple* $\frac{12}{4}$ *compound*

$\frac{2}{8}$ *simple* $\frac{3}{4}$ *simple*

Activity 3.2—In-class activity

Fill in each measure below with notes that correspond to the requested time signature. Be creative with combinations of note values that fit each time signature.

Answers will vary.

(a) $\frac{4}{8}$

(b) $\frac{3}{4}$

(c) $\frac{4}{2}$

(d) $\frac{2}{4}$

Activity 3.3—In-class activity

Using numbers, the syllables "&," "e," and "a," write in the counting for exercises below. Make sure you know which note value gets the beat.

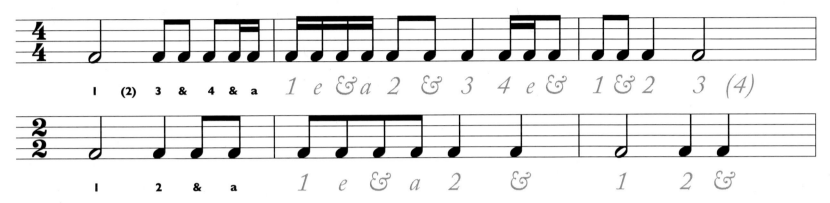

Activity 3.4—In-class activity

Get together in groups of three and clap the rhythms below. Each student will practice clapping his or her line individually. Once everyone understands their lines of rhythm, all three students will clap their lines simultaneously with each other. This may be hard at first, but practice it until you are able to clap your line while the other two students are clapping their lines. Write in the counting for each line.

Chapter 4

Activity 4.1—In-class activity

Give the number of beats in each measure for the following compound meters:

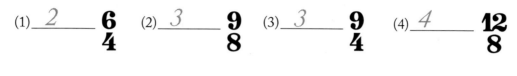

(1) __2__ **6/4**　　(2) __3__ **9/8**　　(3) __3__ **9/4**　　(4) __4__ **12/8**

(5) __3__ **9/16**　　(6) __2__ **6/8**　　(7) __4__ **12/16**　　(8) __2__ **6/16**

Activity 4.2—In-class activity

Circle the words or syllables that you emphasize when you sing this song. Circle the notes that occur on the beats.

Row, Row, Row Your Boat

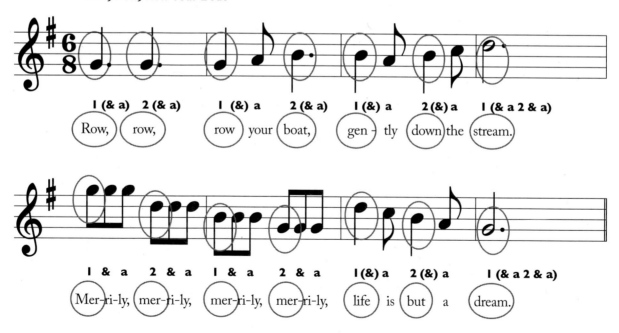

Chapter 5

Activity 5.1—In-class activity

Using the paper keyboard in the Helpful Tools section, determine the exact notes of the following major scales using the major scale pattern of whole tones and half steps. Have one student start with the first note and then have another student give the next note of the scale in descending or ascending order. Continue this exercise between the students until the scale is completed with the octave.

a) **D** major scale   D   E   F♯   G   A   B   C♯   D

     remember: W   W   H   W   W   W   H

b) **A** major scale   A   B   C♯   D   E   F♯   G♯   A

c) **E** major scale   E   F♯   G♯   A   B   C♯   D♯   E

d) Choose a major scale and fill in the notes of that major scale:

Answers will vary.

Chapter 6

Activity 6.1—In-class activity

Refer to your Circle of Fifths chart to answer the following questions:

TUTOR TIP

Just by looking at the Circle of Fifths chart, you can come up with many different questions about scales, keys, flats, and sharps. We recommend doing this especially if the students are taking a while to provide correct answers.

a) How many sharps does the key of E major have? _*4*_

b) How many flats does the key of A♭ major have? _*4*_

c) Which notes are flatted in the key of E♭ major? _*B♭, E♭, and A♭*_

d) Which notes are sharped in the key of A major? _*F♯, C♯, and G♯*_

Chapter 7

Activity 7.1—In-class activity

Use the blank staff to complete the following:

a) Write a treble clef on the blank staff and include the key signature of D major
with a time signature of $\frac{4}{4}$.

b) Write the D major ascending scale on the staff with quarter notes (be sure to use
measures appropriately). Begin with the D above middle C.

c) Above each note, write the correct scale degree number, including the caret above
each number.

Activity 7.2—In-class activity

Use the blank staff to complete the following:

a) Write a treble clef on the blank staff and include the key signature of G minor
with a time signature of $\frac{4}{2}$.

b) Write the G natural minor ascending scale on the staff using half notes (be sure to
use measures appropriately).

c) Above each note, write the correct scale degree name. Remember, the key is minor.

Activity 7.3—In-class activity

Transpose the given melody from the key of A♭ major to the key of B♭ major on the
blank staff below. Remember to use the five steps discussed earlier.

Step 1: A♭ major

Step 2:   1̂ 7̂   3̂ 4̂ 5̂ 7̂   6̂ 5̂ 7̂   1̂

Step 3: B♭ major

Step 4:   1̂ 7̂   3̂ 4̂ 5̂ 7̂   6̂ 5̂ 7̂   1̂

Chapter 8

Activity 8.1—In-class activity

Identify the size of the intervals below.

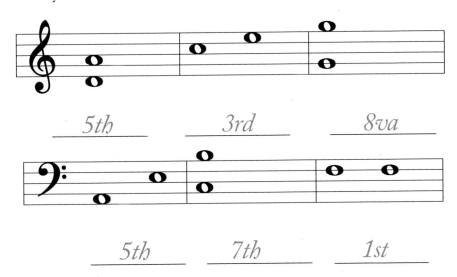

5th   3rd   8va

5th   7th   1st

Activity 8.2—In-class activity

Using what we have learned about interval size and quality, identify the intervals below.

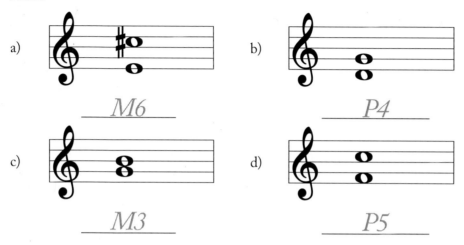

a) ___M6___

b) ___P4___

c) ___M3___

d) ___P5___

Activity 8.3—In-class activity

Using what we have learned about interval size and quality, identify the intervals below. Remember to use the key of the lower note even if that differs from the given key signature.

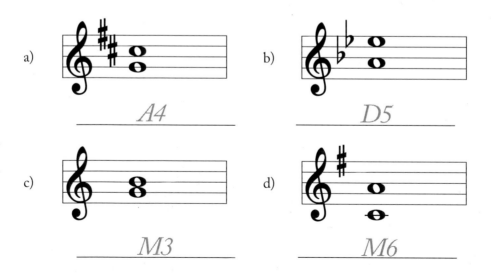

a) ___A4___

b) ___D5___

c) ___M3___

d) ___M6___

Chapter 9

Activity 9.1—In-class activity

Using the given note as the root, build the following triads. Begin by inserting a generic third and fifth, then apply the appropriate sharp or flat to create the quality indicated.

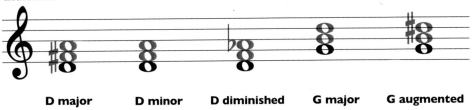

D major   **D minor**   **D diminished**   **G major**   **G augmented**

Activity 9.2—In-class activity

Use the given note as the root to arpeggiate the major triads in Figure 9.10a and the minor triads in Figure 9.10b. Finish each measure by adding extra notes or changing note values to fit the meter. If you add an extra note, be sure that the note is in the same major or minor triad. Answers will vary but must include the correct triad notes and four beats per measure.

Figure 9.10a

Example: D major triad   *G major*   *F major*   *B major*   *A major*

Figure 9.10b

Example: E minor triad   *A minor*   *D minor*   *G minor*   *C minor*

Chapter 10

Figure 10.7 Ascending and descending arpeggiated triads

Activity 10.1—In-class activity

Which four triads are being represented in the arpeggios notated above? Get in groups of two to discover the triads expressed in the measures in Figure 10.7. Write your answers by giving the name of the triad (e.g., G major).

a) Measure 1 = *A minor*   b) Measure 2 = *E minor*

c) Measure 3 = *C major*   d) Measure 4 = *D major*

Activity 10.2—In-class activity

Give the analysis with Roman numerals of the triads in Figure 10.7. Get in groups of two to discover the triads expressed in these measures. Write your answers with Roman numerals, including the correct capital or lowercase numeral indicating major or minor. Figure 10.7 is in the key of G major.

a) Measure 1 = *ii*   b) Measure 2 = *vi*

c) Measure 3 = *IV*   d) Measure 4 = *V*

Chapter 11

TUTOR TIP
Both of these activities
may be hard for the
students. Have them
take their time and
if they are still strug-
gling, write different
triads on the board with
different key signatures
in order to give them
more practice. Reassure
them that this kind of
analysis takes time to
fully understand.

Activity 11.1—In-class activity

Make the following root position triads into first inversion triads in the blank
measures on the right. Include the Roman numeral and inversion number.

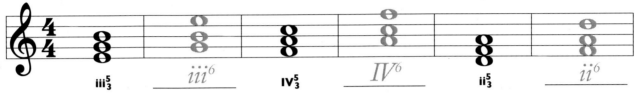

Activity 11.2—In-class activity

Change the following root position triads into first and second inversion triads in the
blank measures on the right. Include the Roman numeral and inversion number(s) on
each triad.

Chapter 12

Activity 12.1—In-class activity

Use the "implied" notes for each pair of notes below by labeling the notes with the correct type of triad. Note the key differences in each measure.

TUTOR TIP

Make sure students are using both the bass and treble clefs together to analyze the types of triads.

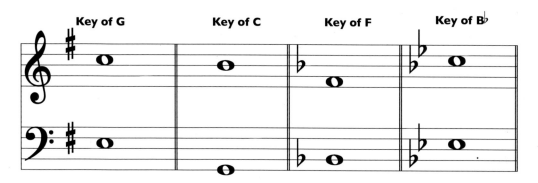

Triad: *C major (IV)   G major (V)   B♭ maj (IV)   C minor (ii)*

Activity 12.2—In-class activity

Finish analyzing the excerpt in Figure 12.5 by labeling groups 3 and 4 with the correct Roman numeral analysis. Students may work in groups of two.

Group 3: Notes in group   *E*   *B*   *G*   *E*

Triad name   *E minor*

Roman numeral in key of G   *vi*

Group 4: Notes in group   *D*   *B*   *F♯*   *B*

Triad name   *B minor*

Roman numeral in key of G   *iii*

Activity 12.3—In-class activity

Finish labeling the Roman numerals below with the correct inversion type.

TUTOR TIP

This activity may be best to do in pairs. Remind the students that they are "investigators" and they are analyzing what the piece is telling them about the notes they see.

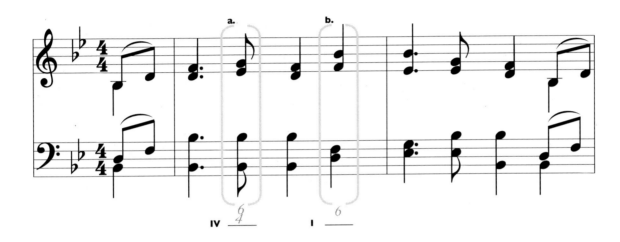

Supplemental Material Activity S.1

Write out the minor scales indicated. Remember, you should always begin with the natural form of the minor scale and make adjustments (such as a raised seventh degree scale) as needed.

A harmonic minor

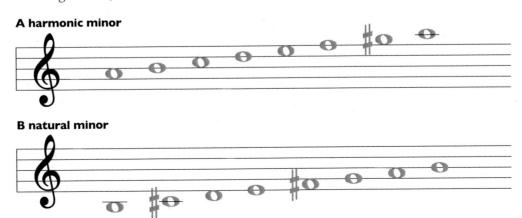

B natural minor

Supplemental Material Activity S.1 (continued...)

Write out the minor scales indicated. Remember, you should always begin with the natural form of the minor scale and make adjustments (such as a raised seventh degree scale) as needed.

G melodic minor

C harmonic minor

Glossary

accent mark. A stress or emphasis placed on the note (Ch. 12).

accidental. A sharp, flat, or natural symbol to the left of a note. In the context of key signatures, the temporary alteration of a pitch (Ch. 1, 6).

adjusted interval. An interval where the higher note is outside of the major key or scale of the lower note (Ch. 8).

anacrusis. A note (or notes) that occurs before the first complete measure; also referred to as a "pick-up note" (Ch. 3).

arpeggio. Notes of a chord that are broken up and played one after another in sequence (Ch. 9).

augmentation dot. A symbol (·) placed after a note or rest, increasing the value of the note or rest by half (Ch. 2).

augmented interval. An interval where the top note of a major or perfect interval is raised by one half step (Ch. 8).

augmented triad. A triad built with the major third and the augmented fifth (Ch. 9).

bar line. A vertical line that separates one measure from another on the staff (Ch. 3).

bass clef. A symbol (𝄢) used to notate pitches that are to be played on a lower pitched instrument or with the left hand on a keyboard (Ch. 1).

bass note. The lowest-sounding pitch in a chord (Ch. 11).

beam. A horizontal line, used in place of flags, that connects groups of notes together to represent a single beat (Ch. 3).

beat. The fixed, rhythmic pulse of a piece of music (Ch. 3).

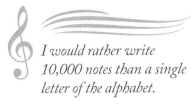

I would rather write 10,000 notes than a single letter of the alphabet.

—Ludwig van Beethoven

chords. A harmonious group of notes that can be played together or separately (Ch. 9).

clef. Characters set at the head of the staff to indicate the pitch or position of the notes (Ch. 1).

close harmony. Notes of the triad placed as close together as possible (Ch. 11).

compound interval. An interval with a size of more than an octave (Ch. 8).

compound meter. A meter in which the beat is divided into three equal parts (Ch. 3, 4).

diatonic triads. Triads that use only the notes, including sharps or flats, of a given scale (Ch. 9).

diminished interval. An interval where the top note of a perfect or minor interval is lowered by one half step (Ch. 8).

diminished triad. A triad built with the minor third and the diminished fifth (Ch. 9).

dominant. The fifth scale degree, considered the second-most important scale degree behind the tonic scale degree (Ch. 7).

double bar. The double bar line shows that the piece is over or that there is a major shift in the overall idea of the piece, such as a key or time signature change (Ch. 12).

duple meter. A meter (simple or compound) characterized by a group of two beats per measure (Ch. 3, 4).

eighth note. A note written with a filled-in note head and a stem with a single flag always written to the right of the stem. Two eighth notes make up a quarter note (Ch. 2).

enharmonic equivalents. Two notes that have the same pitch or tone but have different names (Ch. 1).

enharmonic equivalent key signatures. Two scales with the same sounding notes that can be called by two different names (Ch. 6).

fermata. A symbol (⌒) used to show the note should be held longer than the normal note value. The duration is usually up to the musician's discretion (Ch. 12).

first inversion triad. A triad where the third of the triad is the lowest (bass) note (Ch. 11).

flat. A symbol (♭) used to indicate the note is lowered a half step (Ch. 1).

grand staff. In sheet music, treble and bass clef staves that are joined together (Ch. 1).

half note. A note written with an open note head and a stem either extending up or down from the open note head. Two half notes make up one whole note (Ch. 2).

half step. The shortest distance between two notes (Ch. 1).

harmonic interval. Two notes played at the same time (Ch. 8).

harmonic minor scale. A scale based on the natural minor scale that raises the seventh scale degree by a half step (Supplemental Material).

interval. The distance between two notes or two pitches (Ch. 8).

interval quality. The specific type of relationship between two notes. It can be minor, major, perfect, diminished, or augmented depending on the interval size (Ch. 8).

interval size. The number of lines and spaces, or letter names, represented on the staff (Ch. 8).

inverted triad. A triad where the notes are rearranged so that the root is no longer the lowest sounding pitch (Ch. 11).

key (musical key). The tonal center of the music (Ch. 6). See Musical key (Ch. 6). See Scales (Ch. 5).

key signature. The organization of flats and sharps shown at the beginning of the staff that indicates in which key the music is written (Ch. 6).

leading tone. The seventh scale degree; only one half step down from the octave tonic in the major scale (Ch. 7).

ledger lines. Lines used to show notes that go higher or lower than the five lines of the staff (Ch. 1).

major scale. A series of eight notes that begins and ends with the same note, an octave apart, and follows this pattern of whole steps (W) and half steps (H) in ascending order: W–W–H–W–W–W–H (Ch. 5).

major triad. A triad built with the major third and the perfect fifth (Ch. 9).

measure. A singular grouping of beats (Ch. 3).

mediant. The third scale degree; the very middle note between the tonic and dominant scale degrees (Ch. 7).

melodic interval. An interval in which one note occurs after another note (Ch. 8).

melodic minor scale. A scale based on the natural minor scale but raises both the sixth and seventh scale degrees by a half step (Supplemental Material).

melody. A series of single notes used to express a musical idea (Ch. 7).

meter. The specific beat groupings and divisions that occur within music (Ch. 3).

middle C. On the grand staff, it is the first ledger line below the treble clef and the first ledger line above the bass clef. On the piano, it is the key near the middle of the keyboard, with twenty-three white keys to the left and twenty-eight white keys to the right (Ch. 1).

minor interval. An interval where the top note of a major interval is lowered by one half step (Ch. 8).

minor triad. A triad built with the minor third and the perfect fifth (Ch. 9).

musical key. A specific set of pitches used to create a piece of music; the scale around which the music is centered (Ch. 6).

natural. A symbol (♮) used to cancel out either a sharp or a flat to indicate that the note is in its natural state (Ch. 1).

natural interval. The major and perfect intervals represented in the major scale (Ch. 8).

natural minor scale. A series of eight notes containing this specific pattern of whole steps (W) and half steps (H) in ascending order: W–H–W–W–H–W–W (Ch. 5).

natural notes. The notes A, B, C, D, E, F, and G. Natural notes repeat themselves in alphabetical order up and down the keyboard. On a keyboard or piano, the natural notes are the white keys (Ch. 1).

notate. To write music on a staff (Ch. 5).

note value. The specific duration of a note (Ch. 2).

octave (8*va*). The distance between two notes with the same letter name (Ch. 1).

open harmony. Harmony in which the notes of the triad are spread more than an octave (Ch. 11).

pitch. The attribute of a musical tone produced by the number of vibrations generating it (Ch. 1).

quadruple meter. A meter characterized by four beats per measure (Ch. 3, 4).

quarter note. A note written with a filled-in note head and a stem either extending up or down from the note head. Two quarter notes make up one half note (Ch. 2).

relative key. Pairs of major and minor scales that share the same key signature (Ch. 6).

relative minor scale. The minor scale of a key that uses the same sharps and flats as a major key (Ch. 5).

repeat. A symbol (:‖) used to signify that the musician should repeat the musical phrase immediately before the repeat sign (Ch. 12).

rest. Requires a specific time of silence using symbols that correspond to note values (Ch. 2).

rhythm. The passage of pitch through time (Ch. 2).

Roman numeral analysis. A form of harmonic analysis where Roman numerals are used to represent different chords in a given score (Ch. 10).

root. The foundational note on which a triad or chord is built (Ch. 9).

root position triad. A triad where the root of the triad is the lowest (bass) note (Ch. 11).

scale. A series of musical notes organized by ascending or descending pitches (Ch. 5).

scale degree. The name or number of a note in a scale (Ch. 7).

second inversion triad. A triad where the fifth of the triad is the lowest (bass) note (Ch. 11).

seventh chord. A chord comprised of a triad (root-third-fifth) plus the seventh above the root (Ch. 12, Supplemental Material).

sharp. A symbol (♯) used to indicate the note is raised a half step (Ch. 1).

simple interval. An interval within an octave of the starting pitch (Ch. 8).

simple meter. A meter in which the beat is divided into two equal parts (Ch. 3).

sixteenth note. A note written with a filled-in note head and a stem with two flags that are always written to the right of the stem. Two sixteenth notes make up one eighth note (Ch. 2).

slur. A curved line between two different notes indicating the notes are connected and should be played smoothly (Ch. 12).

staccato. Detached, separated; denoting a style in which the tones played are more abruptly disconnected (Ch. 12).

staff (plural, **staves**). The five lines on which musical notes are written (Ch. 1).

subdominant. The fourth scale degree, right below the dominant scale degree (Ch. 7).

submediant. The sixth scale degree; the "lower mediant" of the scale, falling in the very middle between the subdominant and higher tonic scale degrees (Ch. 7).

subtonic. The seventh scale degree, a whole step down from the octave tonic in the natural minor scale (Ch. 7).

supertonic. The second scale degree, one whole step above the tonic (Ch. 7).

tie. A curved line connecting two notes of the same pitch that are to be sounded as one note equal to their combined note value (Ch. 2, 12).

time signature. The vertical stack of numbers placed at the beginning of the staff immediately following the clef to indicate the meter (Ch. 3).

tonality. The principle of organization of a piece of music around a tonic (Ch. 10).

tonic. The most important note of a scale, which gives the scale its name; the first scale degree of a scale; the tonal center of a scale (Ch. 5, 7).

transposition. The process of rewriting notes at a higher or lower pitch, also involving a change in the key signature and pitch, but not the time signature or rhythm (Ch. 7).

treble clef. A symbol (𝄞) used to notate pitches that are to be played on a higher pitched instrument or with the right hand on a keyboard (Ch. 1).

triad. A three-note chord written in thirds consisting of the root, third, and fifth (Ch. 9).

triple meter. A meter (simple or compound) where each measure contains three beats (Ch. 3, 4).

unison interval. An interval in which successive notes lie on the same line or space in a given staff (Ch. 8, see Figure 8.3).

whole note. A note written with an open note head that does not have a stem. Two half notes make up one whole note (Ch. 2).

whole step. The distance of pitch equal to two half steps (Ch. 1).

(also I don't understand what its purpose is.)

(what I would change about this course

1. goes too fast and it doesn't dig deep enough for you to understand the concept.

2. hard to learn music without sound and a book doesn't make sound so it isn't learning piano, but you are expected to understand. ☹?